EGE AT ORMSKIRK.
STEPHEN WILKINSON F.R.I.B.A. COUNTY ARCHITECT PRESTON.
C000260556
SECTIONS AND ELEVATION TO ASSEMBLY HALL
TO QUADRANGLE

# A Vision of Learning

Edge Hill University 1885–2010

# A Vision of Learning

## Edge Hill University 1885–2010

by Fiona Montgomery and Mark Flinn

Picture Acknowledgements

Most of the images come from the Edge Hill archives and modern photo bank. Edge Hill and TMI Publishers would like to thank Mike Nolan for access to images on his 125 blog as well as all the photographers who have contributed. They would also like to thank the following people and organisations for allowing material to be reproduced: p30 water colour reproduced by permission of John Harvey; p36 *Mary Evans Picture Library*; p38, p46 *Topfoto* and p48 *Getty Images*.

A Vision of Learning: Edge Hill University 1885–2010



First published in 2010 by
Third Millennium Publishing Limited,
a subsidiary of Third Millennium Information Limited.

2–5 Benjamin Street
London
United Kingdom
EC1M 5QL
www.tmiltd.com

**ISBN 978 1 906507 48 0**



Project managed by Susan Millership
Designed by Susan Pugsley
Production by Bonnie Murray
Reprographics by Studio Fasoli, Italy
Printed by Printer Trento, Italy

# Contents

# Preface

The first two editions of the *History of Edge Hill College*, published in 1985 and 1997, provided a rich account of the development of the institution from its early days in Durning Road to the turbulence of the early 1990s. The subsequent period has seen the rapid development of the institution, and the achievement of taught degree-awarding powers, research degree-awarding powers and University title. The authors were commissioned to update the history of the University in celebration of its 125th anniversary in 2010. We have attempted not only to describe the academic, physical and social development of the institution over the years, but also to explain the backcloth of regional and national policy changes that have influenced, but not driven, its development.

The authors are grateful to many people who have given of their time and expertise. In particular, they would like to thank colleagues who helped to locate many of the book's images, in the University Archive and elsewhere: Sam Armstrong, Roy Bayfield, Helen Miles, Caroline Mitchell, Mark Molloy, Jill Palmer who assisted with typing and Joan Steele. Mike Nolan, whose 125 blog provided a running commentary during the anniversary year, deserves particular thanks. Many others have given generously of their time in providing reminiscences, by commenting on drafts and by correcting errors of fact: Tanya Byron, John Cater, Chris Coleman, Seth Crofts, Rhiannon Evans, Oliver Fulton, June Gibbons, Steve Igoe, Ruth Jenkinson, Bill Johnson, Alistair McCulloch, Lesley Munro, Anne Richards, Sue Roberts, John Simons, Robert Smedley, David Tomkins and Bob Wilson.
Thanks are also due to all who helped with previous editions.

*Fiona Montgomery*
*Mark Flinn*

# Foreword

It has been a challenging journey. It has encompassed the days before the opening ceremony in 1885, when the Board of Education refused to ratify the stone-carved name of Liverpool Undenominational College; through the change from philanthropic support to local authority control and the move to Ormskirk; to the sequestration as a wartime hospital; the James Report and the 1970s closure of teacher training colleges; the proposed merger with the then Lancashire Polytechnic; the switch from county council ownership; the failure to obtain university status under the 1992 Further and Higher Education Act; and, eventually, another opportunity under the 2004 Act, to degree-awarding powers and University title.

Mark Flinn and Fiona Montgomery chart this course with clarity, insight and enthusiasm. Both are well placed to do so. Professor Montgomery is a leading women's historian, the author of *Edge Hill University College, A History 1885–1997*, which deals with the earlier period in greater depth, and was a leading member of staff of the University throughout the last two decades of the 20th century. Mark Flinn was an outstanding Pro Vice-Chancellor (Academic) from 1992 until his early retirement in 2009, and, so often, the author and the pilot of the institution's destiny. We are delighted they were prepared to be so generous with their time and expertise in producing a book of which both they and the University can be justifiably proud.

Now 125 years on, it is timely to reflect on and celebrate what our forebears and my current colleagues have achieved. Edge Hill is now a successful and vibrant university with the capacity to become an ever-more significant provider of life chances to the people we serve. It is a privilege to be a small part of this success, and we are eternally grateful to those whose contributions, past, present and future, make Edge Hill University a place and a community of which we are justly proud.

*Dr John Cater*
*Vice-Chancellor*

*Overleaf: Edge Hill Western Campus.*

CONCILIO
CONSILIUM
125

FoH

Faculty of Education

1

# Beginnings 1885–1920

On 7 February 1882 seven Liverpool businessmen and philanthropists – Alexander Balfour, Thomas Matheson, Samuel Smith, William Crosfield, WP Sinclair, S McDairmid and SG Rathbone (Chairman of the Liverpool School Board) – concerned about the lack of non-denominational training for teachers, met to found Edge Hill, the first non-denominational Teacher Training College in England and Wales. A Committee was established, which, after tireless fund raising, secured a large house in Durning Road. This was furnished, adapted and enlarged at a total cost of £16,483 of which over £10,000 was met by subscriptions. It was formally opened at a large meeting in St George's Hall, Liverpool by the Rt Hon. GD Trevelyan MP and Dr JG Fitch, the Senior Inspector of Schools, on 24 January 1885.

### Staff

Edge Hill began with a very well-qualified staff. Sarah Jane Yelf was appointed Principal. Trained at Salisbury Diocesan Training College (1861–2), she became headmistress of Teddington Church School on completion of her course and remained there for three years. From 1868–76 she was second mistress at Salisbury College and then appointed Inspectress of the Liverpool Board Schools and Principal of the Liverpool Pupil Teachers' Centre for Girls. Appointment of a woman principal was far in advance of official thinking; it was not until after 1904 that regulations required a woman principal for a women's college. Harriet D Feuchsel, previously a governess at Brighton Technical College became First Governess; Mildred Fenemore, former headmistress of St Michael's Girls' School, Highgate, Second Governess; and MK Dewhurst, the Third Governess, came straight from Derby Training College. Mrs Evans taught cookery and a number of visiting lecturers came for subjects such as drawing and music.

### First students

In July 1884, 100 candidates took the Queen's Scholarship Examination and from these, 41 were admitted at the end of January 1885. Edge Hill's intention was 'to produce a superior class of Elementary School Mistresses', thereby trying to create the impression that they were a cut above the ordinary training colleges.

In listing admission qualifications, Edge Hill rated health first. Teaching was seen as an extremely tiring occupation, and one for which a woman needed to be very fit. Then came position on the Queen's Scholarship list; character testimonials; ability in drawing and science; and a rather vague 'every other circumstance from which or may probably be inferred that the

*Sarah Jane Yelf, first Principal.*

*The College's first premises on Durning Road, Liverpool.*

advantages bestowed in the College will lead to the desired result'. A good knowledge of French, German or Latin was 'desirable', while skill in needlework, domestic economy and music was 'indispensable'. Edge Hill, therefore, was reflecting and reinforcing conventional gender roles with its emphasis on stereotypical skills such as needlework and domestic economy.

Students were required to bring a waterproof cloak, two pairs of stout walking boots, galoshes or rubbers, two pairs of shoes, a dressing gown, flannel underwear ('vests at least'), a white or cream dress, navy blue serge dress for school and classroom, aprons, two toilet covers and two bags for linen. For PE, one cream and one crimson shirt blouse in 'Delaine' fabric, made with 'yoke, turn down collar and full sleeves with loosely fitting cuffs' was required. (By 1912, PE kit had changed to 'knickers, tunic and jersey', which had to be bought from Edge Hill 'to ensure uniformity'). A sailor hat with College band and badge was compulsory for weekday wear. Students were 'expected to appear at all times neatly and becomingly attired'. Teeth were to be 'put in order' and revaccination undertaken. All this represented a formidable financial outlay and must have been very off-putting for the poor, but bright, girl. Furthermore, the student also had to pay her fees: £10 for those who had been pupil teachers and had first-class Queen's Scholarships; £12 for those in the second class. If the student had not been a pupil teacher, fees were £15 for the first-class scholarship holder and £20 for the second.

### Curriculum

College syllabuses followed broadly the same lines as the Queen's Scholarship Examination, though in more depth. Students studied practical teaching, reading and recitation, arithmetic, music, grammar, literature, geography, history, and, reflecting conventional thought, maths for boys and needlework for girls, and, in addition, school management. Specialisation was not envisaged, the aim being to produce a *class* not a *subject* teacher.

*Early Hockey.*

## Improvements

Any deficiencies detected by Her Majesty's Inspectors were quickly remedied. The sleeping accommodation, criticised in 1886, was improved to the HMI's satisfaction by 1887. On 10 September 1889, it was stated that more sitting room was needed for both students and governesses and that the institution needed redecoration. Within a month, 50 writing tables and armchairs had been ordered, and by February 1890, a scheme proposed to erect a new wing with a day room on the ground floor and accommodation for 13 on the first floor. The extra space released would be used to give the governesses a sitting room. The cost was £2,000. Work was begun on 9 September 1890 and completed on 30 September 1891. An even quicker response came in October 1890; Dr Fitch, the HMI, suggested that an additional governess should be appointed to teach drawing. Within *four* days it had been agreed to appoint one.

Under Yelf's leadership, Edge Hill quickly established itself in a position of strength. By 1890 it was in the first class. Yelf's health however was not good and she was forced to retire in 1890 aged 44 (though she did live to the age of 83!). The Committee asked Dr Fitch, the HMI to recommend a suitable successor and, at his suggestion, Sarah Jane Hale was offered the post. The decision was taken before the application of Miss Feuchsel, who had been acting principal, was even considered. One can only infer that Miss Feuchsel was treated rather shabbily.

## Miss Hale's Principalship 1890–1920

Miss Hale began her career as a pupil teacher, then studied at Whitelands Training College. She was

*Students in the North Cloister, Edge Hill, Liverpool.*

*Sarah Jane Hale, the College's second Principal.*

headmistress of two elementary schools, at the first of which (a London slum school) she met Matthew Arnold who was then an HMI. She soon moved to St Katherine's College Tottenham as First Mistress. While at St Katherine's, she decided that she needed more academic training to do full justice to the job so she resigned and went to Newnham College, Cambridge, where she took a third in Mental and Moral Science. Her next appointment was as Method Mistress at Cheltenham Ladies' College. She had had therefore, more experience than Yelf, though no doubt Matthew Arnold's friendship also helped. Whatever the case, Edge Hill had secured a very able Principal whose tenure proved to be a time of consolidation rather than radical change.

### Development 1890–1906

In 1890 the government established Day Training Colleges. This led to changes in the syllabus of residential colleges, which could now take up university work and give certain students a third year of training. Geography, history and domestic economy became optional in Year 2, and science or language could be studied instead of, or in addition to, the ordinary subjects in the curriculum. In drawing, students received either a First- or Second-Class Drawing Certificate according to ability in freehand, model, light and shade, and geometrical drawing. Blackboard drawing was no longer compulsory. At Edge Hill, botany was introduced in 1891, mechanics in 1892 and physiography, maths and physics in 1893.

### Day Students

Edge Hill did not welcome the idea of day students. Five students were reluctantly admitted at the beginning of 1892. Their homes had to be within a convenient distance of the institution and they attended Edge Hill from 8am to 8pm, following the same curriculum as the resident students, the only difference being that they slept at home. Later generations of day students certainly did not feel part of the community, as Catherine Campbell (1932–4) recalled: 'We were never really accepted by the rest of the College and our only "home" was a cloakroom which we called "Clint" [Clint Road being adjacent]. We were rather like displaced persons.' Day students ceased with the move to Ormskirk in 1933, when Edge Hill became fully residential.

*An early production of* King Lear.

### Year 3 University Students

From 1894 students of sufficient calibre were able to read for university degrees. Initially students prepared for London matriculation, classes were then started for the Victoria Preliminary, which led to affiliation to Victoria University, Manchester. Next, they moved to Liverpool, where Edge Hill lecturers were recognised as teachers of the University so that students could spend their first year at Edge Hill. After three years they received a degree plus a professional certificate from the Board of Education. Edge Hill was very proud that, 'of all the women's colleges, [it] has hitherto prepared the largest proportion of its students for degree courses'. This proved an aid to recruitment: Ethel M Ryley (1919–21) 'chose Edge Hill because, along with Homerton, they were the only two colleges which combined teacher training and a degree course'. The practice of a non-university sector playing a role in degree teaching therefore has long antecedents.

### Accommodation

Accommodation was to prove a continuing problem and one which was only solved for a six- year period between 1933 and 1939. The premises were enlarged in 1893 by renting two adjoining houses and the kitchen improved in 1894. Although this meant 110 students could now be accommodated, it was not a long-term solution. Plans were drawn up for a new extension and appeals made for subscriptions. The

Marquis of Londonderry, Lord President of the Council and President of the Board of Education opened the new wing on 31 October 1903. It provided three new classrooms, two laboratories, a library and gymnasium. Despite two additional dormitories, some students still had to sleep out. Edge Hill could now take 160 students. However, even with subscriptions, a debt of £7,000 remained. A Bazaar held in St George's Hall, Liverpool, 4–6 October 1906 raised £3,976, of which £3,900 went to reduce the debt.

In 20 years, Edge Hill had almost quadrupled its student numbers, enlarged its premises and dealt successfully with all the changes in government legislation. Glowing HMI reports highlighted its success. An example from 1901 is typical: 'This is one of our most successful Colleges; 75 per cent of the second years had "double firsts" in the Class List.'

### Development of Teacher Training 1902–1914

Prior to 1904, the Board of Education formulated training colleges' syllabuses, prescribing a uniform curriculum for each subject. After 1904, colleges could draw up their own schemes providing they conformed to a general outline laid down and approved by the Board. Students were taught the subjects needed in a secondary school since these were also considered relevant to the primary. This meant a great increase to the number of subjects: the second-year student had to take English language, literature and composition, history and geography, elementary mathematics, elementary science, hygiene, theory of music, principles of teaching, reading and repetition, drawing, needlework, singing and physical training. Hale felt 'optimistic', seeing 'possibilities … for development and progress'.

In 1907 the Preliminary Examination replaced the King's Scholarship entrance examination for the Certificate. This was in two parts: Part One, composition and arithmetic; Part Two, English, history, geography plus one option (elementary science, mathematics or a foreign language). Candidates would not be graded into classes, though those passing any of the Part Two subjects with credit received a distinction. Hale saw this as an attempt to lower standards, discourage working for a university degree during a training college course and separate primary and secondary schools. To increase applicant numbers, Entrance Examination standards were to be lowered. Colleges now had little effective choice of candidates and the 1907 entry was 'distinctly below the ordinary College standard'. This was a bitter blow since Edge Hill had been used to attracting the academically able. Its students had regularly out-performed the entrance standards of the male students at Cardiff University.

Hale also proved correct that the increase in training colleges (an additional 11 by 1908) and places (up from 7,000 in 1903 to 12,000 in 1910) would lead to unemployment. Thirteen per cent were unemployed at the end of 1908 and nearly 40 per cent in 1909. The position began to level out after 1910 and World War I ensured there was no shortage of positions. Hale suggested that the Board of Education should pressurise Local Education Authorities to employ trained teachers instead of the untrained ones who were often preferred on grounds of economy. In Lancashire only 16 per cent of teachers were trained or certificated, while 23 per cent of male and 32 per cent of female trained teachers were unemployed. This oversupply of trained teachers would lead to lower salaries, lower status and, ultimately, lower qualifications.

In 1913 the number of subjects to be taken was

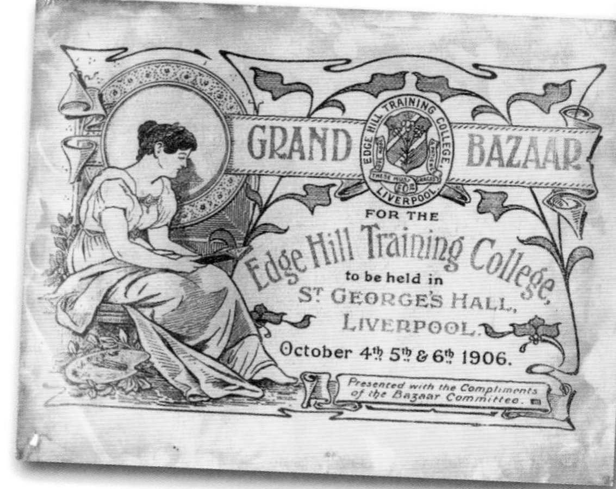


*Ticket to the Grand Bazaar that raised funds for the College in 1906.*

EDUCATION DEPARTMENT.

TEACHER'S CERTIFICATE.

THE LORDS OF THE COMMITTEE OF THE PRIVY COUNCIL ON EDUCATION

Hereby Certify That in the month of July, 1897

Emily Martha Randell

having been a Student during two years in the Edge Hill Training College was examined for a Certificate and placed in First Division of Candidates of the Second Year.

Also that the above-named Candidate served the required period of probation in the Hull Craven Street Higher Grade Board School.

This Certificate qualifies the Teacher to Superintend Pupil Teachers.

Date 6th June 1897

Vice-President

TWO YEARS OF NORMAL TRAINING SUCCESSFULLY COMPLETED

*Third Year Students, 1907.*

reduced, with more time given to professional subjects. Subjects were grouped into three classes: Professional (compulsory) – principles and practice of teaching: hygiene, physical training, theory of music and singing, reading and recitation, drawing, needlework; General Studies – three, or in special cases two, from the following – English, history and geography, maths, elementary science; Additional subjects – taken by those aiming to improve their general education – French, German, Latin, physics, chemistry, botany, rural science and housecraft. This helped the weaker student and met with Hale's approval.

## Patterns of Student Recruitment

### *Origins*

Edge Hill was designed to be a national, rather than a local, institution. In terms of origin 1885–1920, however, students came overwhelmingly from Lancashire in general and Liverpool in particular. Apart from 1893 and 1902, more than 80 per cent of all students came from the neighbouring counties of Lancashire, Yorkshire, Cheshire and Cumberland. Edge Hill was essentially an institution of the North West. Equally, although designed to cater for the needs of non-Anglicans, only in 1893 did the percentage of Anglicans fall below 37 per cent, while in ten of the years between 1887 and 1920, Anglicans formed over 50 per cent of the student intake. The typical student was aged between 19 and 21 and had, till 1907, been a pupil teacher. In 1907 the bursary system was introduced and thereafter most students were bursaried.

### *Destinations*

Except for 1897 and 1911, Lancashire and Yorkshire took over 70 per cent of Edge Hill's certificated teachers with Liverpool itself usually securing over 20 per cent. Furthermore, more than 50 per cent usually returned to their home town and a number even to the same school, while of the remainder, many moved within the same county. This was normal, as the *Board of Education Report* 1912–13 commented '… many students, especially women students, desire to obtain posts in or near their homes, and hesitate to accept appointments in some unfamiliar or distant part of the country'. Even unemployment did not force students to move. Hale disapproved strongly: 'It is regretted that seven have felt obliged to accept appointment as uncertificated teachers rather than go out of Liverpool'.

The College's 25th Anniversary, 1910.

The graduates, however, were prepared to move, and sometimes relatively long distances, eg from Blackburn to Horsham. By 1907 there had been 96 graduates – 66 BA and 30 BSc. Lancashire employed less than half of these (in contrast to the non-graduates) and Lancashire, Cheshire and Yorkshire together took 69 per cent. As might be expected, the more academic graduates did tend to secure rather more prestigious jobs though this was not a uniform trend: in some years the type of employment acquired was very similar to that of the non-graduates. Of the 96 graduates, 12 had become lecturers (three were in post at Edge Hill), three were HMIs, three science mistresses, one first assistant and the vast majority (72) were assistant teachers. Despite the large number of science graduates (30), only three had jobs as science mistresses.

### Salaries

Initial salaries were as follows: Yelf, £200 a year; First Governess Harriet Feuchsel, £90 with three £10 increments to a maximum £120; Second Governess, Mildred Fenemore, £70 with two £10 increments to £90; Third Governess, Miss Dewhurst, £60 by £5 increments to £80.

By 1896 staff consisted of the Principal, First Governess and five resident governesses. The First Governess now started at £120, received two increments of £5, then two of £10 to a maximum of £150. The position of the governesses however had not changed, and in some respects had worsened, since with increments restricted to £5 a year it took longer to reach their maxima. Their starting salaries ranged from £55 to £70 and the maximum from £80 to £90. Governesses were not allowed to do outside work and were to work an eight-hour day. Mrs Evans, the housekeeper and cook, a trained teacher who taught cooking, started on £80, increasing by £5 increments to £100.

The salaries for the governesses do not appear over-generous and indeed, when Fenemore resigned in 1886 to get married, the Committee wished to engage a replacement starting at £75 a year. Yelf, however, reported that she was finding difficulty in attracting anyone at that rate and the Committee agreed that £80 could be offered 'if necessary'. Miss Tucker was

Miss Dewhurst,
Third Governess.

appointed at the higher figure.

The Principals fared better. Yelf's salary was £200 a year. When Hale replaced her in 1890, she received £250, which by 1910 had been increased to £400, together with board and lodgings worth a further £85. Miss Cunnington was appointed as the first Vice-Principal in December 1905 at a salary of £120 and only held the position for six months before resigning in June 1906. Miss JA Jenkins replaced her at a lower salary of £100 (this became standard Edge Hill practice: whenever someone left an attempt was always made to employ a cheaper replacement). This was increased from 1 September 1907 to £120 with two increments to a maximum of £150. Thereafter rises came quite regularly and by 1918 she was receiving £250 plus board and lodging worth £65. Over this period therefore her salary increased from approximately half that of the Principal to two-thirds. When Acting Principal, however (October 1909 to April 1910), Jenkins received only a bonus of £63.

Although a rudimentary system of salary scales was adopted, there appears no discernible reason for the way in which these were used. By 1909 the Finance Committee had some misgivings over automatic yearly increases, preferring that they should determine pay. Those who were entitled to automatic increases were to continue to receive them until their maxima were reached, then it was up to the Committee. Accordingly many got nothing in 1909. Salaries were revised annually though not everyone benefited; the average increase was £5 but Hale received £50 in 1910 while Jenkins received only £10. In 1914, because of the financial state of the country no one was to get a rise except Gowland, who was awarded £10.

From 1 September 1920 the Burnham scale was adopted, bringing a degree of uniformity. Miss Smith, who had started on £500 from 1 September 1920, immediately enjoyed £700, while her full salary in 1922 was reckoned to be £800. National scales were paid from then on. This meant that Smith received more in 1922 than the Professor of International Politics at Aberystwyth did in 1931.

The Art Room.

## World War I

War seemed to touch the internal workings of Edge Hill little. In the *Report* of 1914–15, Hale maintained that, 'A sympathetic and intelligent interest in current events has been stimulated by literature dealing with the war, its causes and probable effects, and by addresses, notably one given by a Belgian lady, Madame Biemé, on Belgium, and another by an Alsatian, the Counte [sic] de Croze, on Alsace'. Not all of this, however, fell on receptive ears: interest in current affairs was not a noted characteristic of the average Edge Hillian: 'I [Edna Walker 1915–17] do not remember either buying or seeing a paper so we were not aware of the stupendous events in Gallipoli, nor the collapse of Russia, nor Zeppelins over London, nor the use of the war-winning weapon, the tank'.

Nevertheless, the students were aware that their existence might seem very self-contained:

> *It may seem to those who read the following pages [of the* College Magazine*] that the Great War has made little or no difference to us, but that is far from being the case. In addition to the numerous 'War Works' which had been carried on by all with unabated energy and enthusiasm, there* **is** *a difference in the very attitude of mind brought to bear on the ordinary things of life … There are such big things at stake that material interests count for little in comparison.'*

To help the war effort Hale urged all to buy War Savings Certificates and encourage thrift. Edge Hill twice entertained soldiers from a local hospital to a 'gorgeous feast'. Relations were somewhat strained because 'the soldiers were shy; until a regrettably vulgar comic from their midst lowered the tone, but raised the spirits of the entire gathering. I can still see Miss Hale's face with that "we are not amused" expression. After that, however, things went with a bang and the soldiers danced and sang with the students and really enjoyed themselves.' A second occasion proved a 'flop'. Food was provided for 70 but only seven turned up, a local cup-tie proving more attractive. 'But for the hungry students it was a Field Day' (Edna Walker 1915–17).

Women were now increasingly needed to teach boys, and students did teaching practice in boys' schools. Hale, however, was not happy: '… one does not contemplate with satisfaction the dearth of men teachers. However well the women teachers succeed in the management of boys, they need more of virile quality to make them really efficient, especially for the older scholars.' This was in marked contrast to her views of 1895:

> *It is terrible heresy, no doubt, and would lead to a great upheaval in the present order of things, but why also should not a woman teacher be paid at the same rate as a man? She does the same kind of work, puts in more rather than less, hours per day, and may be as highly certificated.*

> *Even when she is working under precisely the same conditions, say as Assistant in a boys' department, her salary falls very much below that of her fellow-assistant, just because he is a man, and for no other reason.*

War brought financial hardship; by 1918 Edge Hill was 'greatly relieved' that the Treasury grant was to be increased, 'for in spite of raising the entrance fee and of ultra economical management on the part of our invaluable Mrs Evans we were likely to find ourselves in a tight place had not this addition come most opportunely'.

Physical conditions were deteriorating; the autumn of 1918 saw a water shortage, leaking pipes, the heating breaking down and a flu epidemic in September with another in February 1919. It was becoming increasingly obvious that the institution needed to expand and it was planned to extend the Clint Road wing to give more classroom space, dormitory accommodation and more suitable quarters for staff. Hale appealed to old students to contribute.

Academically there was one major alteration during the war years. In 1915 two grades of papers – 'Ordinary' and 'Advanced' – in the Required Subjects were introduced. Subjects, previously known as 'Optional', were now called 'Additional'. A 'pass with credit' was available in the Required Subjects and a 'pass with distinction' in Advanced and Additional papers. This gave an incentive to the good student to work hard and Edge Hill approved.

Hale greeted The Fisher Education Act of 1918, which now *inter alia* raised the school leaving age to 14 and made larger grants to local authorities to enable them to increase teachers' salaries, with enthusiasm: 'There are many signs that the nation is awakening to the value and importance of Education, and to the fact that not only is the labourer worthy of his hire, but is himself worthy ... when it becomes effective it should do much towards establishing Education on sounder and more complete lines than heretofore.'

Several of the proposed changes had already been adopted at Edge Hill eg the University of Liverpool examined students for their Certificate instead of the Board of Education. This had worked quite satisfactorily for nine years except for the financial side, since Edge Hill was responsible for all the expenses. From 1919 the University's Senate Training College Committee and the Board of Education were to approve syllabuses, examination papers and final results in a system which covered Edge Hill, Warrington and Chester Colleges. This was to cost each institution £100 a year.

By the end of Hale's principalship, Edge Hill had come a long way. It was firmly established as an institution of the first rank. It had trained 2,071 girls of whom by 1920, 213 were Head Mistresses, 178 First Assistants and 30 science mistresses. She had guided the institution for 30 years – a period that had seen much political turmoil and a World War – and gave Edge Hill a presence on the national stage through her work with government committees.

Undoubtedly Hale had great presence; most of the students stood in awe of her. Edna Walker (1915–17) remembered in 1978:

> *Miss Hale was a very great lady: to most of us a remote and powerful presence, yet to anyone in real distress she could be infinitely kind. Her mental capacity and her ability to deal with the many difficulties that wartime brought were without parallel. She was really an old lady, 66 years old when I left College, but neither her demeanour nor her dress showed it. There was never any doubt that she was 'The Principal'.*

She was nevertheless retiring at the right time; it is doubtful whether at her age she could have coped with the problems of the post-war world. It was unfortunate, however, that she died on 1 April 1920 *before* her well-earned retirement began. Many tributes of appreciation paid testimony to the respect and loyalty that she inspired and a large number felt that their 'loved and esteemed Head would have preferred her call to the Higher Life to come as it did while she was still in harness'.

# To Ormskirk, Bingley and Back

2

Hale's successor was Miss EM Smith, who had an impeccable academic record. Educated at Newnham College, Cambridge, where she took a First in mathematics and achieved a position equal to the 16th wrangler, she then spent a year in the United States as Fellow in Mathematics at Bryn Mawr College. On returning to England she became maths mistress at Cheltenham Ladies' College, (1910–16) and then Headmistress of Rotherham Municipal High School (1916–20).

Smith was faced with dealing with debt – despite increasing fees to £25 and receiving a larger grant from the Board of Education, 'a very large burden of debt … hangs heavily around our necks, and it is not yet clear how it can be removed'; government cuts, which again caused unemployment for graduating students, as well as a reduction in student numbers to 153; and a building no longer fit for purpose.

### A New Campus

There were constant problems with the boilers and other items of costly maintenance. What was needed was an entirely new College, although the cost would be prohibitive. In 1925, however, the Board of Education Report condemned the building and site. A new building in a new location was needed which would require state assistance in the shape of a local authority. The Committee decided to hand over Edge Hill to Lancashire County Council on condition that it provided a new building as soon as possible, and preserved the original name, history and reputation. The new governing body included many of the old Committee and kept as its Chair, Mrs Charles Booth. Lancashire became tenants of the Durning Road site at a nominal rent. The Chair of Lancashire Country Council, JT Travis-Clegg sent a warm letter of welcome to Guild members through the *College Magazine*. This was no mean bargain for Lancashire: it was acquiring a well-established college at a time when it was highly unlikely that the Board of Education would agree to an entirely new creation.

*The new buildings included an Assembly Hall, an indoor swimming pool and the Hale Memorial Hall.*

*Stone carving above the College's main entrance commemorating the official opening of the Ormskirk campus in 1933.*

The existing building, however, still caused costly problems: in 1928 the institution was re-wired at great expense and it lacked adequate heating. Indeed, students used a rudimentary heating duct to get rid of the dust from their cubicles: 'we … swept the bits down a grating which ran down the centre of the corridor. This was supposed to be for a kind of central heating but as no heat ever came up we used it for dust. So with no other heat it was terribly cold in the winter' (N Aldred, 1925–7).

The new campus consisted of 34 acres on the present site in Ormskirk. Smith reported delightedly: 'When I first saw it, hares were disporting themselves upon it, and I like to think of the rural aspect which this gives to what will be our surroundings.' Unspoken fears of the isolated nature of the place were dispelled when it was found to be only 15 minutes from the station 'and omnibuses run in all directions … Southport, Wigan, St Helens and Liverpool are within short distances, so that we shall not be cut off too much from the amenities of the city and from a variety of schools'.

Travis-Clegg laid the foundation stone on 26 October 1931. The new buildings were a prime example of 1930s architecture and consisted of a main education block, four halls of residence, each to accommodate 50 students and four staff, and a dining hall for 250. The education block housed an Assembly Hall, library, craft rooms, gymnasium, music rooms, lecture and classrooms. The Trustees of the Old College provided an indoor swimming pool and the Guild gave £1,500 to decorate the College Hall to be known as the Hale Memorial Hall (Hale Hall). The halls of residence were named Stanley, Clough, Lady Margaret and John Dalton 'in honour' of the Derby family and 'of three individuals famous in the history of Lancashire and of Education' (Ann Jemima Clough was a pioneer of higher education for women, having founded Newnham College, Cambridge). The students played a full role in developing and laying out the extensive grounds.

Lord Irwin, President of the Board of Education opened the building on 2 October 1933. Speakers emphasised educating the *whole* individual: 'we want in our teachers vivid personalities in healthy bodies, able to enjoy all kinds of physical activity, and we want also sensitiveness to beauty and to the dignity of simple, orderly living'. It was 'more important to teach people how to think than what to think' and 'children and adolescents must be trained to enjoy their leisure time

*Postcard showing the College's new facilities, 1930s.*

also with pleasure and profit'. Edge Hill now consisted of 180 students with four resident maids for each hall.

The Durning Road premises were eventually purchased by Liverpool Education Department for £6,000, the net proceeds used to pay for the swimming pool. A German bombing raid on 28 November 1940 scored a direct hit on the building, causing it to collapse into the cellars below where around 300 people were sheltering. This caused the boilers to burst and 166 people died of scalding or drowning. Churchill described it as the 'worst single incident of the war' as regards domestic loss of life.

### Academic changes

From 1921, university students were to spend a fourth year at Edge Hill; this was to be used for their professional training to reduce the strains of preparing for both Finals and teaching qualifications. Edge Hill was now in line with the universities.

In 1929, final examinations became the responsibility of an examination board representing the universities and training colleges. External examiners were appointed and the first examination under the new system took place in 1930. The Board of Education paid £1.50 per candidate and the student

College badge.

£2.50. Smith feared that the fee could not cover the cost.

Edge Hill proceeded cautiously; the only change it proposed was to allow students to offer two subsidiary or professional courses instead of one ordinary course. All students already took such courses in their first year but previously these had not been formally examined. The proposed subjects were to be mathematics, geography, history and science.

The results of the first examinations proved 'quite satisfactory' with two fails, 21 distinctions, 53 credits and 54 passes. Smith now looked on the new system more favourably: 'We see a tendency to increase the number of tests, and we may expect to see a raising of the standard of requirement for passing. It is of course in the interest of the nation that the qualifications of its teachers should be as high as possible.'

The Depression's effects on education continued throughout the 1930s. In response to a fall in the school population and the increasing tendency to employ cheaper, less-qualified teachers, the Board of Education continually reduced college admissions from 1932–5 and one applicant in three did not secure a place. Reductions in Edge Hill's admissions meant that a building designed for 200 had only 166 students. Unemployment also remained a problem with a large number only securing temporary appointments. This in turn affected recruitment, particularly in 1937 when Edge Hill had 41 vacancies.

CLASS TIME TABLE.

School Loraine St (Infants) Class..........

Mornings.

| Day. | 1 | 2 | 3 | 4 |
|---|---|---|---|---|
| M. | Reading | Singing | Number | Phys. Ex. Writing |
| T. | Reading | Number | Nature | Phys. Ex. Crayon Dr. |
| W. | Reading | Singing | Number | Phys. Ex. Writing. |
| T. | Reading | Number | Nature | Phys. Ex. Writing. |
| F. | Reading | Singing | Number | Phys. Ex. Writing. |

Afternoons.

| Day. | 1 | 2 | 3 | 4 |
|---|---|---|---|---|
| M. | Reading. | G. Needlework. B. Handwork | Story | Phys Ex. Crayon Drawing. |
| T. | Word Building + Language. | Free cutting. Recitation | Story | Handwork + Games & Exs. |
| W. | | | | |
| T. | Word Building + Language | Games & Exs Drawing. | ~~Recitation~~ Story | Paper work + Dramatisation. |
| F. | Reading. Geog | G. Needlework B. Handwork. | Paper work Hdw | Clay + Optional. |

Class timetable, 1921.

*Winners of the Drama Cup, 1935.*

## The Years at Bingley

Edge Hill spent World War II sharing Bingley Training College in Yorkshire. Ill health and increasing sight difficulties forced Smith to retire at the end of the summer term, 1941. Miss Butterworth was appointed Acting Principal at a salary of £400 for the duration of the war.

The Edge Hill timetable was tailored to fit Bingley commitments so that both colleges could use the classrooms, the gym and the field. This enabled usual programmes to be followed and college societies to function. Lectures were also held on Saturday mornings.

Wartime brought its own problems: insufficient schools for teaching practice, limited transport and a lack of suitable applicants. Numbers had been limited to 160 for the period at Bingley, but by 1942 Edge Hill had only 138. By 1943 students could enter college at 17+ instead of 18+. Almost half of those admitted in 1944 were under 18, which meant that they did not have to have the Higher School Certificate. Butterworth in the *Newsletter* repeatedly lamented the lack of the 'right sort of candidate'. Not all were committed to teaching. At 18 a girl was liable for national service and some chose to take up teaching (a reserved occupation) to avoid this. The shortage of domestic staff meant that students had to do an ever-increasing amount of domestic and household tasks for themselves. Butterworth optimistically told the Governors in 1942 that the students were enjoying their 'Housewife' turns. However, Mary Bancroft (1943–5), looking back in 1969, probably sums up the students' reactions more accurately:

*Visit to Rushworth and Dreaper museum, 1928.*

*Edge Hill spent the war years sharing Bingley Training College in Yorkshire.*

*Apart from cleaning our own rooms (banging threadbare mats on the steps on Saturday mornings), twice a term one would have a day on "housework" with one's room-mate. We were excused lectures while we swept and dusted, cleared the tables and set them again, doled out tea and buns in the afternoon and milk in the evening. Housework was not very popular but even less so was work in the main kitchens which was necessary once for a few weeks when there was a strike of kitchen staff. Oh, those horrible pans to scrape and piles of lettuce to wash and search for caterpillars, but the kitchen work was only temporary, thank goodness.*

At one point the students 'proclaimed a strike against sharing household chores, and had to be reminded that the only alternative was a visit to the Labour Exchange to be drafted into factories'.

The vacations were spent doing national service: everything from fruit picking to munitions, hospital work to war nurseries. Red Cross activities continued throughout: in 1945 they gave £146 for POW parcels and the two colleges raised a total of £602 between 1941 and 1945.

In preparation for the move back to Ormskirk in spring 1946, an extra 51 students were admitted. They spent the autumn teaching in their local areas and became resident at Ormskirk in January 1946. Numbers were further increased to 280 for the 1946 session. The temporary buildings (the 'Huts') constructed during the war (and of which one is still in use) were adapted to make students' rooms, classrooms and a hall for resident domestic help 'whom we still hope to find'. New courses were to be provided: A housecraft course limited to 32 students was designed to produce teachers to cope with problems caused by raising the school-leaving age. The students would take Housecraft

*Architect's watercolour of College entrance, Frank Waddington, 1931.*

as their Advanced Subject and spend a third year in a Domestic Science College; General Science and Social Studies were added with a lecturer from Liverpool University's Social Science Department helping in the setting up of the latter.

Much work was needed to restore Edge Hill to civilian use. The floors were 'so black that a London firm had to be called in to restore their natural oak colouring'. The kitchens lacked 'machinery', the furniture needed reconditioning and the building redecorating. Nevertheless in 1946, Butterworth stated that the buildings were 'almost as beautiful as they were before the war'. Removal took place on 24 January. A full assembly for prayers was seen on 15 February. The realities of the post-war world were in evidence though not yet fully appreciated: all students had to take turns at domestic work and many staff also helped in the kitchens. The resident maids had gone forever. Throughout this period a willingness to make the best of things was apparent and the speed with which Edge Hill returned to normal was remarkable.

The increase in numbers to 280, however, meant that conditions were very cramped: first years lived two to a room for almost the whole session; the new rooms for housecraft were not ready so 'they practised at first on the staff sitting-rooms, and began upholstering some of the chairs damaged during the war'. There were still insufficient schools for teaching practice.

Butterworth had proved an auspicious choice for Principal; she was universally liked and her personality did much to ensure a relatively smooth running of the institution in the difficult conditions of evacuation. Finding a successor to her posed problems. The first advertisement threw up no suitable candidate; the re-advertisement, however provided Edge Hill with its best-qualified Principal yet. Margaret Bain had a first-class Honours degree from Aberdeen University, a doctorate from Paris and 14 years' university teaching (three at Cardiff and 11 at Edinburgh) as well as school experience. It was fortunate that such an able woman had been secured, since her principalship was to see Edge Hill develop from a small, women's establishment to a large, mixed institution.

# 3 The Student Experience

Edge Hill, like other female training colleges, promoted a culture of femininity and control. Refinement was one of its goals as the HMI Report of 1895 stated: 'the surroundings of the students are calculated to refine their mind and manners'. Students had to come from 'a suitable home environment' and display 'alertness, pleasantness of manner, responsiveness, some amount of individuality, a real desire for the work… No lethargic, stolid, unobservant, unattractive – whether in speech or manner – or unsympathetic person, however physically strong, mentally well-equipped, and even morally sound should be accepted for the teaching profession'. Dress was to be demure at all times. At PE in the 1890s they wore 'thick blue serge tunics buttoned up to the neck and with long sleeves, and "bloomers" ... to match. Over the outfit, even in the summer, we had to put on our dress skirts, for it was considered indecent to show even our ankles. What shapeless bundles of humanity we must have looked, and how hot we were in summer' (Agnes Sutton, 1893–4). Even from 1904 – when Edge Hill was the first to adopt the new Swedish system of gymnastics, and gym kit now consisted of a navy blue dress with a red sailor collar in which 'the whole body was free to move as Nature intended, and the hems were a whole eleven inches from the ground!!!' – once PE was over, normal dress of voluminous skirts with tightly boned corsets was resumed.

*In 1904 Edge Hill adopted the Swedish system of gymnastics.*

Replicating the middle-class home and family was central to notions of femininity. At Edge Hill, a system of 'mothers and daughters' prevailed, whereby second year student 'mothers' supervised their 'daughters' during their first year of socialisation into College life. This was a general system at the time. Unlike other colleges, however, it did not cease at Edge Hill with the advent of male students in the 1960s, but simply encompassed 'fathers and sons' and continued till the 1980s. Meal times were also an instance of the way in which the dominant norms of middle-class society were transmitted. The midday meal, 'dinner', was the formal one with staff in attendance and the Principal's personal maid waiting behind her chair.

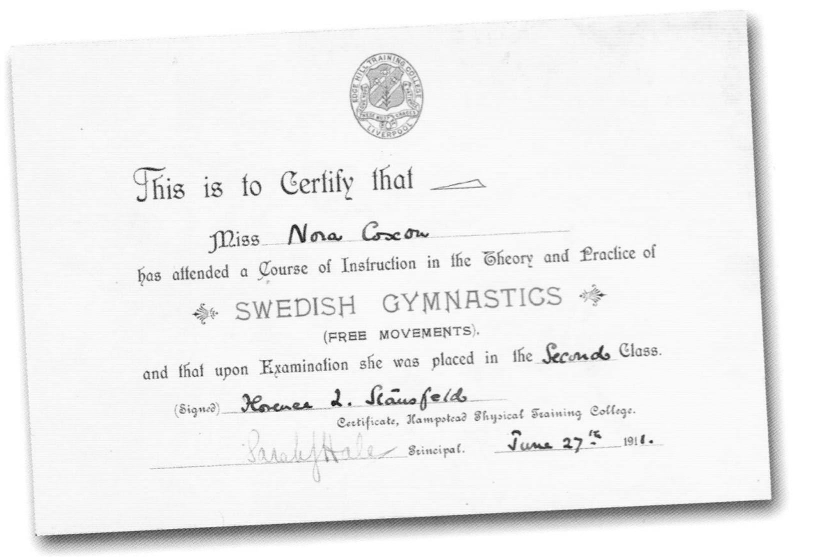

This is to Certify that

Miss Nora Coxon

has attended a Course of Instruction in the Theory and Practice of

SWEDISH GYMNASTICS

(FREE MOVEMENTS),

and that upon Examination she was placed in the Second Class.

(Signed) Florence L. Stansfeld

Certificate, Hampstead Physical Training College.

Sarah J Hale Principal. June 27th 1911.

*Students in the gymnasium and dining hall in Liverpool.*

Domestic duties, considered light by the standards of the time – the HMI, Fitch commented in 1888 and 1889 that he was glad that Edge Hill students had not as much household and laundry work as those in other colleges – consisted of fetching and carrying their own washing water, tidying their rooms and certain meal duties.

Students were split into two groups; each in turn received instruction morning and afternoon in class or did schoolwork, cookery, industrial work and private study. Four to six students were 'morning servers'; between 9am and 10am they cleared tables, washed cups, saucers and plates. They then studied till noon when they set the tables for dinner and waited. This was a nerve-wracking experience for the new student:

> *The unfortunate victims had to rush to the dining room, fight for a dozen knives, forks, spoons with which to set the table (always somebody was without the required number and appeals to the kitchen were ignored!). Others helped prepare the meal, while a third set checked that the bathrooms were in order. Afternoon servers saw tables were cleared and set for tea while afternoon cooks had "easy duties" which lasted only till 3pm and consisted mainly of the concocting of dainty dishes. (Mary Shepherd 1909–11).*

Control was maintained by strict supervision. To create teachers with the correct sense of duty who would become agents of social control, students were subjected to a spartan regime designed to keep them busy all day: 'The routine was inflexible – we slept, ate, worked and took walks, attended lectures and church and fulfilled extraneous duties from which no excuse could be contemplated.' This contrasted with the experience of university students who did not have to account for every minute of the day.

The weekday was unusually long. It began at 6.15am when the rising bell was sounded and finished at 10pm with lights out.

Chorus of the College Song, written in 1907 by Maud Mitchell.

| | |
|---|---|
| *6.15am* | *Rising bell* |
| *7am* | *Prayers* |
| *7–8am* | *Classwork (seniors)* |
| | *school, study, cookery, (juniors)* |
| *8–9am* | *Breakfast and tidying of rooms* |
| *9am–12 noon* | *Classwork* |
| *12–12.30pm* | *Recreation* |
| *12.30pm* | *Dinner* |
| *2.30–4.30pm* | *Classwork (juniors)* |
| | *School or study (seniors)* |
| *4.30pm* | *Plain tea* |
| *5–6pm* | *Walk* |
| *6–8pm* | *Private study* |
| *8.30pm* | *Supper* |
| *9pm* | *Prayers* |
| *9.45-10pm* | *Silence (designed for private prayer)* |
| *10pm* | *Lights out* |

Out of the 15 hours and 45 minute-long student day, only two hours and 15 minutes were designated for recreation.

There was however a certain disquiet about the heavy workload: in 1894 the HMI commented, 'The timetable shows a heavy amount of mental work, and a comparatively slight amount of time for private study and recreation'. And two years later (1896) it was still causing concern: 'Efforts will no doubt continue to be made to secure a substantial respite from study for every student in the course of the day, which is all the more important because the College does not possess very extensive grounds for the Physical Exercise of so many young persons.' (HMI Report 1896.)

The emphasis throughout was on order and control, on creating a shared culture with carefully prescribed roles, norms and values. The governesses constantly supervised the girls during the working day; while the senior students were responsible for enforcing discipline during recreation times and special monitors were in charge of dormitories. Students were responsible for seeing that all windows were shut before bedtime. If one were found open, a governess would wake up the person on window duty to close it, again demonstrating who was in control.

Students were not allowed to leave the premises after 5pm on weekdays. Saturday afternoons were free but permission was required to go off site and they had to return by 7pm (except in special circumstances). Saturday nights were modelled on family entertainment with the students sewing at the feet of the Principal while she read aloud from an 'interesting

Left: Students enjoying a picnic.

or instructive book'. Student societies (apart from the games clubs) were designed to be of a highly improving nature. During meetings, students made clothes for poor Liverpool children to have at Christmas, reflecting traditional ideas of service to the less fortunate. Saturday evening lectures, open to former students and friends and of an improving nature, were introduced in the autumn of 1891.

Sundays were relatively free. After breakfast, Hale gave a talk known as 'meditation'. This was not popular, as Norah Howie (1907–9) recalled: 'Most of it was above my head and to judge by faces around me, to many others too.' Each student then had to attend the church of her denomination (though the College was non-denominational students were required to attend daily, morning and evening prayers). At the 8pm roll call students had to answer 'once' or 'twice' signifying the number of times they had been at church. Those replying 'once' had to explain why. Every minute of the day therefore was strictly accounted for.

Restrictions also extended to accommodation. All students were entitled to a cubicle (known as a 'cube') partitioned by wooden panels ending about four to five feet from the ceiling. This gave very little privacy 'for every sound could be heard throughout the dormitory'. Each cubicle contained a small chest of drawers, a wash-stand, a single bed, a desk and one or two bookshelves. The only light came from one in the corridor which was turned off at 'lights out'; candles were not allowed in the rooms. There was no hot water, only a jug of cold water brought each morning from down the corridor. Students were not allowed to wash in their cubicles between 9am and 9pm but had to use the general lavatory. Baths were taken according to a timetable; each student was allotted 15 minutes and to reach the bathroom had to walk down two corridors and a flight of stairs.

The *Board of Education Report* for 1912–13, commented of training colleges in general: 'The complaint of an old student that they were "sometimes treated like children, sometimes as nuns, sometimes as servant girls", might have been made with equal justice of most boarding schools for young ladies of the day.' Most of Edge Hill's recruits though would have had no first-hand knowledge of boarding schools and, for many, College must have come as a traumatic experience. Edna Walker (1915–17) writing in 1964, however, could not remember 'feeling rebellious at the restrictions'. Others nevertheless, felt that 'the worst of the old system was that in 1904 we were treated as irresponsible beings, and subjected to excessive rules and restrictions' (D Waid).

This certainly seems to have been the case; any attempts at real private study were actively discouraged. 'The most absurd rule I [KW Wild] can remember was that, though we each had a tiny private cubicle, we weren't allowed to use it for study. One of the jobs of the staff on duty was to go poking round

*Helena Normanton, Edge Hill teacher training 1903–5*

Helena Normanton was the first woman to practise at the English Bar in 1922. She was also the first female barrister to lead the prosecution in a murder trial, to conduct a trial in America, and to represent cases in both the High Court and the Old Bailey. She was one of the first two women, along with Rose Heilbron, to become King's Counsel, the highest position awarded to a barrister. She scandalised the legal profession, first by wanting to be part of it, then by insisting on practising in her maiden name. A prolific campaigner for equality within marriage, Normanton was also the first married woman in the UK to be issued a passport in her maiden name. Hailing from Brighton, she trained as a teacher at Edge Hill College, graduating in 1905.

and hustle off any ardent but erring reader. I was too frequently turned out of the very pleasant library.' Miss Wild took first-class Honours in Philosophy from London. This contrasted markedly with conditions for a university student of the same era who could enjoy her own study bedroom and the freedom to work whenever she wished.

There is evidence, however, that students created their own counter-culture. Thus church attendance on a Sunday was used as an excuse for a day out in the country. Students travelled by tram and after 'a few minutes kneeling in the porch of a Roman Catholic Chapel, and possibly being sprinkled with Holy Water', went for a walk, then returned to Edge Hill in time for dinner. Indeed, as late as 1913–15 a Governess was horrified to find that when she 'gave "extension" on Saturday night for students to go the "Pictures", they had meant the Cinema and not the Art Gallery'.

Ethel Annakin – who married in 1904 Philip Snowden, the first Labour Chancellor – used to slip out at night and address meetings of dock labourers. Attempts were made to circumvent the information vacuum in which students lived. Newspapers for example, were not easily available. Mary Sheppard (1909–11) recalled, 'The most daring deed ever done in our year was the opening of a window one Election Night and dropping a halfpenny on a string to a paper boy who tied the "Special Edition" at midnight on to the same string. When we had shut the window we could not read the results – nobody dared to put on the light!'

'Open rebellion' occurred over the food:

*The menu for meals was quite good though not exciting. The cooking at one time was shocking ... Wednesdays and Fridays were known as "Psalm, Fish and Mystery" days because we sang psalms instead of hymns at Morning Prayer and at dinner we had what we called "Mersey Whale" (a whole fish sent to table swimming in a sea of greasy water), and Mystery, a revolting sloppy mixture of flour, bread crumbs, dried*

*A group of Edge Hill students from early in the last century.*

*fruit and huge lumps of suet. On Wednesdays also, one girl at each table of eleven girls would spend a shilling on cake or some seasonable dainty to add to the plain bread and butter provided for tea. Helena Normanton, later famous as one of the first women Barristers, was head girl when she was instructed by the Principal to ask us to forego our cake one Wednesday and give its cost to the Benevolent Fund ... I [KW Wild] was deputed to suggest that Helena should tell Miss Hale that we would rather give up our Wednesday dinner and have the cost of that given to the fund and retain our cake at tea time. Helena did so and Miss Hale was most annoyed that the complaint had not been made before. Henceforth the fish was cooked in an appetising way and very good fruit pudding was served.*

Such improvement, however, seemed temporary, for only a year later KW Wild records 'naked fish ... in a sea of lukewarm water ... What was galling was that years later we were asked to subscribe for a present to the indifferent cooks. I didn't.'

While students were prepared to bend the rules, they endorsed contemporary attitudes to marriage and the family. This was an issue in which Edge Hill took a great interest. Despite the many deficiencies of the College's *Registers* and *Directories* as sources of evidence, there is one piece of information which is always recorded in great detail: the date of a former student's marriage and the number of children she produced. Matrimony therefore was *the* career as far as the staff were concerned; teaching was second best. Edge Hill thus reinforced contemporary mores: a women's *real* place was in the home. This message was also strengthened by glowing reports of gatherings of mothers and children such as this one from 1912: 'There could not be a brighter, happier, healthier looking set of youngsters anywhere and they bear testimony to the fact that Edge Hill has trained good mothers, no less than good teachers.' Teaching, therefore, was a convenient profession for tiding a woman over till she married and by 1920, 34 per cent of its students had married.

Suffragettes speaking in Liverpool, 1908.

Nevertheless, while Edge Hill may have had a clear idea of what a woman's role was – Dr Watson advised graduating students in 1903: 'To men, … make the children keen and quick witted; to women, raise up women to create homes for the men' – and was concerned to propagate this image, the students in their own activities (admittedly held under Edge Hill's aegis) showed a healthy interest in feminism, the suffrage question and other debates of interest to the period. As early as 1894 the College Debating Society decided by 64 to 15 votes 'that the franchise should be extended to women'. However, in 1904 the motion that 'Man's intelligence is superior to Woman's' was surprisingly carried by 41 to 36 votes.

Furthermore, despite Hale's disapproval of feminism in general and the suffragettes in particular, students and former students were interested in getting the vote. As well as debating the proposition on a number of occasions, from 1907 there was a steady reference to suffragette activities in the *Edge Hill College Magazine*. In 1907, Ethel Snowden (née Annakin, 1900–2), contributed an article on 'Education and the Woman Question'. She acknowledged that the *Magazine* was actually publishing it and pointed out that 'politics generally and the woman question in particular' was vitally connected to teaching. It was important to improve mothers' education and home conditions: 'Never a question comes before Parliament but it has some bearing on the sphere which is to be the woman's, the home; or it affects in some way, the woman herself. Yet she has no say in the ordering of her life and that of her children.'

On 25 January 1908 the prospective Liverpool City Councillor, Ellen Robinson, addressed the Guild on 'The Present Political and Social Status of Women' and advocated women's suffrage. In March it was reported that 'College was represented in the audience' at the Picton Lecture Hall to hear Mrs Fawcett and the former Edge Hillian, Mrs Philip Snowden (Ethel Annakin, 1900–2) on 'Women Suffrage'. These speeches 'were listened to with attention by a crowded meeting'.

Two articles were devoted to events of June 1908: Kathleen Ratcliffe wrote on the Hyde Park Demonstration of 21 June and Helena Normanton, (who was one of Edge Hill's most successful university students, having graduated from the University of London with a first-class BA Honours degree in History) wrote on the March to Albert Hall on 13 June. Normanton advocated, 'To all Edge Hill suffragists I give the advice – it takes no moral courage whatever to walk in a procession!' This was an outright call to militancy and contrasted very much with the views of Hale, whose arguments reiterated those of the opponents of women's suffrage. On 23 March 1912, Ethel Snowden gave a 'forcible address on Woman Suffrage' to the Guild and the Home Reading Association meeting 'to an enthusiastic gathering and the discussion which followed proved that keen interest is taken in this subject'. Hale's attitude when women did get the vote was no different: 'It is the duty of every voter to consider carefully what this new privilege means … there is no privilege without accompanying responsibility … the influence of women however felt hitherto … must be exercised for the good of the community as a whole, not in the interest of any one party or sex … '.

Life under Smith reflected the changed times. She took requests for freedom seriously. Given the apprehension on the part of the staff about men coming into contact with the students, it is perhaps surprising to learn that 1924–5 saw the institution of the 'male dance'. Kathleen Beswick (née Bell, 1923–5) 'plucked up enough courage to ask Miss EM Smith, Principal, if we could invite men to our Christmas Dance and if we could wear coloured evening dresses. Hitherto, our evening dresses were all white, and we had had no men for partners. We just danced with each other'. Permission was given and men imported from Chester Training College, two of whom later married Edge Hill students. Guests received a formal invitation and on arrival were marched up and introduced to Smith. 'The Staff were briefed to ensure that couples did not stray beyond the Hall, but I [Catherine Campbell, 1932–4] … managed to get as far as the bicycle shed with my partner only to be discovered by Miss Butterworth with her torch!' It was small wonder that some ex-students described it as 'a convent'.

*Phyllis Hughes in the College garden, 1932.*

Well-qualified herself, Smith had her own ideas about the qualifications needed by intending students. At interview, she told Dorothy Fox (née Elliott, 1938–40) to concentrate on needlework and art. 'To my dismay the comment of the Headmaster was that while Miss Smith ran Edge Hill, he ran Fleetwood Grammar and that I should continue my studies. How glad I have been since that he so advised.'

Mrs Fox saw Smith as '…a terrifying figure. With hindsight one respects her but then one feared her. She always wore long black dresses and walked with a stick. Her black hair was in a bun and because of her bad eyesight she had thick pebble lenses.' Having to sit on the Principal's table was a 'nightmare'. Latecomers had to sit next to her and the 'thought of having to make conversation with her was daunting'.

Despite this the staff were not above making fun of her: 'Miss Barr (PE) was giving us a lecture on posture. She jumped onto the table and imitated various postures ending by imitating Miss Smith's walk. We roared with laughter and the door opened and in came Pip Emma [Miss Smith] to complain about the noise. We wondered how Miss Barr felt up on the table.'

Discipline in lectures was certainly lax: 'It was common practice to knit during the lectures in the large lecture theatre and occasionally there would be the metallic clang of a falling knitting needle. There would be a bustle while knitting was hastily hidden as the lecturer came up the aisle to investigate' (D Fox).

Life at Bingley returned to a more restrictive existence. The rising bell rang at 7am and immediately there was a queue for washing facilities. The solution was either to get up *before* 7am or miss breakfast and wash then. Students were not expected to go out during the week. At the weekends they had to be in by 8pm (extended in the 1944–5 session to 9pm). If a student was going out, she had to write in the Hall Warden's book, stating her destination and the time she was expecting to be back. On dark nights the students had to return in threes. Both staff and students felt ill at ease.

# The Post-War World

4

## The McNair Report

The Board of Education set up the McNair Committee in 1942 to examine teacher training. Its Report (1944) was critical: 'what is wrong with the majority of training colleges is their poverty, and all that flows from it'. To some extent, this was due to size: in 1938 more than 60 colleges had less than 150 students, while only five had more than 200. Edge Hill was above average but not among the largest. To secure adequate numbers of teachers, recruitment should be widened, conditions of service improved with better salaries, and the status of teaching as a career raised. These changes, it was hoped, would enable the country to deal with the 1944 Education Act that raised the school leaving age to 15 and made secondary education compulsory. Specific recommendations included closer association between training colleges and universities, specialist courses in music, arts and PE as well as the introduction of a three-year course, designed to 'foster an academic and social life more akin to that of the universities'.

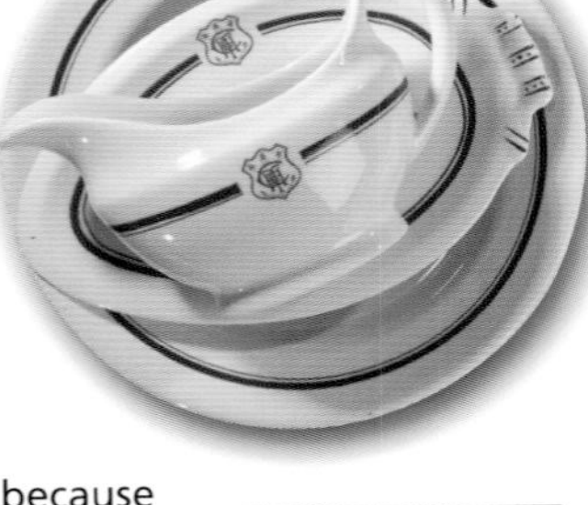

College crockery.

It was, however, easier to plan than to change. The shortage of teachers after 1945 – largely due to the wastage of women teachers because of earlier marriage – meant postponement of the three-year course that was to be introduced in 1960. Edge Hill had no idea what the introduction of the three-year course would mean in reality. The year 1957 saw them first negotiating with the Ministry for additional teaching and improved residential accommodation and then asking for a reduction in numbers to 260.

The Ministry's decision to *increase* the intake in 1959 came as a great shock, especially as it was to be achieved by the admission of day students and the use of hostels as temporary buildings. Edge Hill agreed to increase admissions in 1958 by 15 resident students and to take a further 15 local girls who could live at home. Edge Hill was also to become a *mixed* college of around 400, with the first men arriving in October 1959 and accommodation provided as soon as possible. By October, the College would have 480 students and was enquiring about acquiring extra land. By 1961, a new dining room, kitchen, accommodation for physics, chemistry, general science, biology, rural science, arts and crafts and two new gyms were to be available. Two further women's halls of residence were also planned.

*Left: The first 43 men were admitted in 1959.*

*Principals PKC Millins and Marjorie W Stantan with graduating students: Mr Millins became the first male Principal in 1964. Miss Stantan was appointed Director in 1979.*

Preparations for the reception of male students were soon underway. By 1 September 1959 three men had been appointed to the staff: John E Wilde (PE), TW Eason (education) and A Dawson (physics). Stanley was to be the men's hall of residence. Projected numbers increased from 260 in 1957 to 750 in 1963 and numbers of full-time and part-time staff showed an even greater increase: from 26 in 1956 to 111 in 1967. The dominance of men was quickly established. New appointments tended to be largely male: in September 1961, 13 out of 16 were men. From the initial three of 1959, by 1963 men made up 37 of the 57 full-time staff. And, although female students continued in the majority, female staff numbers declined rapidly: in 1966 there were 27 women to 66 men. The expansion actually meant a *reduction* of employment opportunities for women academics, a position which was reinforced with the appointment of the first male Principal, Mr PKC Millins, a former HMI, to succeed Dr Bain in Summer 1964. This was interesting since there appears no obvious reason, other than positive discrimination, why the introduction of a three-year course and the change to a mixed college should lead to such a transformation. Colleges, which moved from being all-male to mixed, were not inundated with women members of staff.

## Building Developments

By the end of the Autumn Term 1962 the new gym was in use but there was still insufficient teaching space. There was now residential accommodation for 500 in single study bedrooms (a figure which hardly altered over the next quarter of a century); the rest lived at home or in lodgings in Ormskirk.

The new extensions costing £500,000 and consisting of five women's halls (named Lady Openshaw,

*Far left: The new gym was in use by 1962.*

*Left: Synchronised swimming in the College pool.*

Katharine Fletcher (after Chairs of the Governors), EM Butterworth, Margaret Bain (after previous Principals) and Eleanor Rathbone (a noted early 20th-century social reformer and fighter for women's rights), one hall for men (Lancashire), a double gym, dining rooms and an extra science block were finally opened by Princess Margaret on 22 May 1963.

### Academic Changes

In 1960 the National Advisory Council and Ministry of Education recommended a 'balance of training' policy. This assumed that the numbers of primary children would increase at 12.5 per cent but pupils at secondary schools would show only a slight rise. To cope with this, numbers on college secondary courses were to be reduced from 37 per cent to 15 and priority given to maths and science (shortage subjects). This seemed to be relegating colleges to an inferior role, leaving them as the source of non-graduate teachers for infant and junior schools while the universities provided the graduate secondary teachers (as was the position in Scotland). Most colleges avoided this by bringing in 'junior-secondary' courses for the 9–13 age range. Edge Hill agreed to increase the number of primary teachers and those who, though 'trained mainly for secondary work', could also teach in primaries 'without committing itself to rigid proportions'. In practice therefore, the character of Edge Hill's secondary teaching was not markedly changed.

The Newsom report of August 1963 – *Half Our Future* – proposed appropriate training for secondary

*Dancing on the lawn outside Clough Hall.*

*Five new women's halls (Openshaw, Butterworth, Fletcher, Bain and Rathbone) and one men's hall (Lancashire) were opened by Princess Margaret on 22 May 1963.*

modern teachers. Edge Hill quickly took up this challenge and by June 1965 Millins reported that one-term courses for 'teachers of "Newsom" children' were planned to take place between January to March and April to July 1966.

The Robbins Committee on Higher Education, October 1963 proposed a huge expansion in HE with the foundation of six new universities and ten existing institutions gaining university status. In addition, a new BEd degree was to be operated by the Universities' Faculties of Education. Edge Hill, now renamed a college of education, offered the four-year BEd degree of Liverpool University from 1965. Robbins also suggested a further dramatic increase in numbers: 1962–3 saw 49,000 students in 146 colleges; 1970–1 envisaged 82,000 in 156 colleges with a minimum size of 750. This would ensure sufficient resources and a wider range of staff for more specialised courses.

The continuing lack of teachers nevertheless led the National Advisory Council on the Supply and Training of Teachers to recommend in June 1965, increased output from 1965–7 without additional resources. The Wilson Government, with its sights set on technological revolution, accepted the recommendations and the Department of Education and Science published circular 7/65 (July 1965) that called for a 20 per cent increase in student numbers by utilising existing facilities more productively.

By January 1966 Edge Hill's numbers were to reach 750 (including in-service students), which was to be achieved by means of new buildings 'as yet unstarted', reminiscent of Stalin's Five-Year Plans' exploitation of yet undiscovered resources. According to Edge Hill's calculation, it would now be expected to take 985 with an annual intake of 328/9. If they also attracted ten per cent of BEds then there would be a total student population of 1,016 for *initial* training. However, as the postponement of the building programme till 1967 would place a severe strain on tutorial, kitchen

and dining room provision, they did not propose to implement this suggested scheme till September 1967.

Edge Hill suggested a modified form of 'box and cox', ie half-year groups out of the institution for half a term at a time, while a whole-year group would be away for a term during the final teaching practice, giving an Edge Hill year of 36 weeks. With annual intakes of 328 this would mean 956 students in September 1968, and 1,014 by September 1969 (including 10 per cent fourth-year BEd). This would have certain advantages: teaching practice would still be college-based, thus Edge Hill would keep control of professional training; professional and academic studies would receive equal attention; BEd courses would be related to university studies; and it would promote stable community life. Edge Hill therefore intended to play a full part in the DES expansion by 1970.

### The James Report, January 1972

The James Report, *Teacher Education and Training*, January 1972, designed to deal with the mounting criticisms of colleges and fears that given the declining birth rate, they could no longer remain as purely teacher training organisations, recommended three 'cycles' of teacher education: personal, pre-service and in-service training. In-service training was especially favoured and

*'Tomorrow's Teachers' – an illustration from a publication produced in 1963 to promote the institution by Lancashire County Council.*

was to be expanded as 'highest priority'. Colleges and polytechnics should offer new degree courses and a two-year Diploma in Higher Education (DipHE).

Edge Hill responded positively to the 1972 White Paper: *Education: a framework for expansion*. This envisaged a new type of institution encompassing both teacher education and a wide range of BA degree courses. Since Edge Hill met the criteria for an institution specialising in the 'Arts and Human Sciences' and offered a 'reasonable range of advanced courses' for 1,000 to 2,000 students, it hoped to expand to 1,500 students by 1979–80 and to 1,800 by 1983–4, with equal numbers in teacher education and other categories of studies. To attract good quality students it aimed to offer degree courses – BEd [Hons/Ord] and BA [Hons/Ord] – 'from the outset'. The two-year DipHE in practice was relegated to the background.

This required an expansion of staff and buildings including a professional centre, multi-purpose teaching blocks, 'both to replace the huts, built for five years in 1941, and to provide the extra lecture/seminar spaces needed'; Sports Hall, Art/Craft centre, Drama Studio, staff tutorial accommodation, in-service residential block, wardens' accommodation and students' centre. 'At present students' dances have to be held in the dining room: a most unhygienic arrangement'. By

***Jonathan Pryce studied at Edge Hill***

Jonathan Pryce is one of Britain's leading actors and is renowned for his work both on stage and screen.

Jonathan started a teacher training course at Edge Hill when he was awarded a scholarship to study at the Royal Academy of Dramatic Art. After graduation he joined the Everyman Theatre company in Liverpool and became Artistic Director.

From Liverpool he went on to international stardom, appearing in many London stage productions such as *Hamlet* and *The Taming of the Shrew* and his Broadway debut in the *Comedians* gained him his first Tony award. The award winning thespian has also shone in productions of *My Fair Lady* and *Oliver* and won both an Olivier and Tony Award for his first musical *Miss Saigon*.

Jonathan is well known for his role as the villain in the James Bond movie *Tomorrow Never Dies* and has also starred in many film roles such as *Evita*, *Carrington* and all three *Pirates of the Caribbean* movies.

Jonathan has been honoured by his home country of Wales with a BAFTA Special Achievement Award and the 2009 Cymry for the World Honour. In 2009 he was also awarded a CBE for services to Drama.

1985, all that had been acquired was a *non-residential* in-service block through the accretion of Woodlands Chorley, and some minor improvements to wardens' accommodation in the old halls. The huts were still in use, the gymnasium was still under pressure, staff shared rooms and students held dances in the dining room!

## Validation

After 24 years with Liverpool Institute of Education, there was the possibility of a link with either CNAA (Council for National Academic Awards) or Lancaster University. Edge Hill was attracted to the latter, especially since after local government reorganisation in 1974, Liverpool would become part of Merseyside.

Lancaster's known flexibility towards its Colleges of Education, however, and policy of a limited number of colleges undertaking a wide range of work including first degrees proved decisive. Lancaster became the validating body from September 1973, though Edge Hill remained a member of the Liverpool Institute of Education for some of its functions, such as allocation of teaching practice places.

Three major BA degrees – Geography, English and Applied Social Sciences – were instituted in 1975. A further two – History and Combined Social Studies, with a focus on Community Relations (later renamed Urban Policy and Race Relations) – followed shortly. September 1975 saw the first completely *undergraduate* entry (ie entrants had to have a minimum of two 'A' levels). Obviously it was going to be more difficult to attract students since Edge Hill was now competing with universities and polytechnics. It was quite gratified therefore to secure 187 for the BEd and 100 for the BA.

Students still came overwhelmingly from the North West. Indeed, if BEd students were considered within the old county boundaries then there was only a slight change from the late 19th/early 20th centuries, with 82 per cent coming from the North West, Yorkshire and Cumberland. The BAs reflected a slightly wider distribution, but even here 66 per cent came from the traditional catchment area.

*Edge Hill was at the forefront of new media with its own College television.*

Diversification had been the challenge of the 1970s and by a mixture of good luck and good judgement Edge Hill had survived. It had come a long way since the start of Millins' period of office. Millins, however, announced his wish to read for a higher degree at the end of the Summer Term of 1978 and was given a sabbatical year prior to his resignation, with effect from 31 August 1979. The Deputy Director, Miss Marjorie W Stantan, who had had a long association with Edge Hill succeeded him in the interim. She was then appointed Director. Dr Brian Greaves, previously Assistant Principal of City of Liverpool College of HE became Deputy Director.

Stantan had an enormous task in front of her. Colleges were in a vulnerable position. Given that resources for all higher education were limited they had to prove their case for existence against the claims of the much stronger universities and polytechnics. By summer 1981 Edge Hill had borne cuts of a quarter of a million pounds in two years but had acquired Preston Polytechnic's In-Service Teacher Education Unit at Woodlands. Stantan noted: 'the College is now administratively recognisable as an Advanced Further Education institution and looks forward to continued effort in academic and professional fields'. Such optimism was soon to be sorely tried in the shape of a threatened merger with Preston Polytechnic. This aroused fears that should it go ahead, it would 'lead to a loss of University validation, to the transfer of courses to Preston and to the eventual closure of the Ormskirk campus, no matter what guarantees are currently given'. An all-out campaign was mounted and on 27 April 1982 Lancashire Education Committee passed a unanimous resolution that 'the merger be not proceeded with'. There was, however, to be a closer relationship between Edge Hill and Preston Polytechnic, which Edge Hill 'wholeheartedly' supported.

Stantan had been Director for a relatively short time, yet she had faced and overcome immense problems. She had raised staff morale and, when she retired at the end of the Summer Term 1982, a fitting tribute came as Edge Hill was declared 'a centre of excellence' in teacher education in the autumn of 1982. Stantan's successor was Mr Harry Webster, who had held previous appointments at Ulster and Sunderland Polytechnics.

The Smiths played at Edge Hill in 1983.

*Stuart Maconie, Edge Hill 1979–82*

I was asked, 'How does an English graduate end up being a DJ?' I do regard the DJ bit as being a bit of an aberration. I don't know quite how I fell into it – and I don't know when and how I will fall out of it – but the love of literature, and I say this not in a poncy way, though, inevitably, it will sound that way, was instilled in me by the people and things I did here. I chose Edge Hill because it had a great 20th-century literature course and it was here I first got excited about Lawrence, Green, Hardy, TS Eliot and Auden.

Music was one of my main loves when I came here. I remember when I came to take my place in Lancs Hall with my mate Nigel, with our array of musical instruments and the fledgling band we had at the time. We once got kicked out of the music rooms, which had pianos, because we were told they weren't for bands. They were for people to sit and play Debussy's tunes, not for two or three blokes from Wigan to thrash about making a racket. At the time I thought it was the man trying to stop my music but I realise now that it was perfectly reasonable.

Quite soon after I got here, the Hall President, who was a nice Welsh bloke called Dewi, was very into rugger, very into Chris Rea, very into all the kinds of music and things that I, being a lad from Wigan, at the time thought terrible. We once heard about a letter that he had written home which said: 'I was rather hoping for some good fellows to go drinking with who could form a rugby team with me, but all I seem to have got is some punk rockers with electric guitars'. I, of course, thought this was wildly exciting and it made my chest swell with pride.

I saw The Smiths here. This band from Manchester played in the old Refectory, but now I think you realise that it was probably a significant event in the annals of Edge Hill. (For more on Maconie see page 105)

### A Lost Opportunity

Unfortunately, Webster's directorship proved to be a time of lost opportunity characterised by an almost complacent belief in the status quo. The government white paper, *Meeting the Challenge* 1987 and the consequent 1988 Education Act meant that Edge Hill, along with the polytechnics and colleges with 55 per cent or more of their provision at HE level, became independent Higher Education Corporations free from local authority control. Webster was now responsible to a Board of Governors on which business and industry representatives would predominate.

Generally, polytechnics and colleges welcomed this freedom, but at Edge Hill independence was seen as a great challenge and one to which the management did not look forward. They felt well served by Lancashire County Council, and its financial top-up and provision of ancillary services such as payroll had become increasingly necessary. Edge Hill was now to be exposed to the market place with all that entailed. There was no desire

*Above: Students relaxing in the Rock Garden today. Right: The Rock Garden, 1950s.*

to go to CNAA since it was believed that the connection with the University of Lancaster aided recruitment.

All college assets were transferred to the Higher Education Corporations. Edge Hill's main asset was Woodlands, yet it decided not to battle with Lancashire County Council for outright ownership but take the right to use it, without charge, while leaving Lancashire as owner.

Staff had been constantly reassured that life would continue much as before, and it was some time before the realities of independence were realised. There were fears about becoming embroiled in an enterprise culture, which caused problems when Ruth Gee attempted change. Throughout the 1980s Edge Hill underwent a period of consolidation characterised by sound day-to-day administration, but with no real overarching vision and this was no longer sufficient to meet the challenges of the 1990s. Accordingly, the Board of Governors charged Webster's successor, Ruth Gee, with the task of developing Edge Hill so that it caught up with the rest of the sector.

# Ruth Gee's Principalship

5

### The Legacy of the 1980s

Edge Hill College was, by most objective measures, in a weak position on Incorporation in April 1989. Through a long period, best described as 'benign neglect' under the Local Education Authority, there had been no significant capital investment in the Ormskirk estate since the 1971 library building. Much of the teaching outside the original 1933 main building took place in the temporary huts erected during the College's period as a wartime military hospital. Only one new undergraduate programme (Urban Policy and Race Relations) had been added during the 1980s to supplement the long-standing Primary BEd programme and the degrees in English, History, Applied Social Sciences and Geography, introduced in the mid 1970s. The College inherited no financial assets from the local authority. There had been no significant investment for staff or students in information and communication technology. Levels of research activity were very low: a report to the Academic Board showed that there were 21 academic publications by 11 different members of staff in the year 1988. Curiously, for a college substantially engaged in teacher education, there was little serious research interest in teaching and students' learning.

In contrast, the polytechnics and some of the larger HE colleges had used the 1980s to build diversified academic portfolios under the wise guidance of the Council for National Academic Awards (CNAA), and had developed systems and processes that allowed CNAA to devolve quality assurance responsibilities to these growing and ambitious institutions, two of which were within 20 miles of Ormskirk. There were thus enormous challenges facing the new Director.

### The New Director

Ruth Gee was, by her own admission, an unusual, even surprising, choice for Director. She had little experience of higher education, having spent most of her life in secondary schools, though she had been deputy leader of the Inner London Education Authority from 1983–6 and then Assistant Director of North London Polytechnic from 1986–9. She took up post in September 1989, inheriting a conservative, traditional, even comfortable institution that was, however, becoming aware that significant changes would be necessary in order to survive in the new, competitive higher education framework. Her first report to College Governors in October 1989 stated that 'Edge Hill will

*Ruth Gee took up the post of Director in 1989.*

Students in the Union bar, 1980s.

need to adapt and change if it is to continue to survive as a well-respected college of Higher Education.' Gee set out to implement these changes with characteristic energy and determination: her vigorous management style, however, won her both friends and enemies among the staff community and Governors.

### Strategic Plan and Curriculum Development

Earlier in 1989 the new College Governors had approved a Strategic Plan for 1989/90 to 1992/93, which had been submitted to the new Polytechnics and Colleges Funding Council (PCFC). The Plan set out the means by which '...the College will seek to develop further as a learning community which is characterised by excellent teaching, sound scholarship and equality of opportunity for its students and staff'. The Plan set out short-term objectives to:

> *Improve and extend communication; Increase staff and student involvement in decision-making; Increase the sense of corporate identity, and Increase respect for others and the environment in which we live and work.*

Significant among the proposals were plans to develop new undergraduate degrees in Field Biology and Habitat Management, Communication and Media, Organisation and Management Studies, and a range of new Masters programmes in the humanities and social sciences. Bids were made to PCFC for additional student numbers to provide for these programmes.

In the field of education, new secondary Initial Teacher Training (ITT) provision was to be developed, but this took time to materialise and by 1991 the only secondary ITT provision was in the form of four 'shortened' two-year undergraduate degrees for mature students with Higher National Diploma (HND) or equivalent entry qualifications. The Faculty of Teacher Education was thus over-dependent on its Primary programmes: its PGCE and its four-year undergraduate

***Richard Benjamin, BA Urban Policy and Race Relations 1991–4, and Director of the International Slavery Museum (ISM), Liverpool***

I was always unsure of what I wanted to do. I loved archaeology but, when choosing my degree in 1991, I wasn't sure at the time whether I wanted to pursue it.

The course at Edge Hill in Urban Policy and Race Relations really caught my eye – it was definitely the race relations that made me think, 'What's that about?' I chose it over American Studies at another local university, which I was only considering because you got to go to the US!

The idea of studying race relations appealed to me because of my own family background – my dad is from Guyana in South America and my mum is a good old Yorkshire lass from Tadcaster. I was brought up in a town very aware that I was different.

There was a module in African History at Edge Hill. Studying the module was one of those 'epiphany moments', as it was the first time I had explored black and African history. It was very important for someone like me whose ethnic identity was a big part of their life. It's fair to say it was a turning point as pre-1991, I didn't call myself 'black', yet after this module I did – not mixed race, or dual heritage. That was because of the lecturer and the positive way he spoke about black history. He was very influential, as everything I've done since then has been mixed up with the subject, right up to where I am today at ISM.

honours degree, now leading to the award of BA or BSc with Qualified Teacher Status (QTS); the old BEd title was dropped in 1990.

In 1992 the DES Circular 9/92 'New requirements for Initial Teacher Training' set out statutory requirements for the proportion of time that students (now 'trainees') were to spend in schools on practice placements. Universities and colleges would now enter a formal contract with schools in connection with this work, and within a few years the college was paying, in total, an annual seven-figure sum to hundreds of schools in the region and beyond.

Meanwhile, In-service teacher education (as it was then called) continued to develop. Short course provision was modularised and brought within the Postgraduate Diploma framework. A range of initiatives in areas such as Mathematics and Science Education, English across the curriculum in multilingual schools and the establishment of the National Primary Centre, based at Woodlands, maintained a strong college profile.

### Nurse Education and Project 2000

Most significant amongst the proposed developments, however, was an initiative arising from the proposals of the UK Central Council for Nursing and Midwifery (UKCC) in *A new Preparation for Practice* (1986). 'Project 2000', as it was known, set out to integrate the training for nurses and midwives into higher education, through a 'common foundation programme' and a Diploma of Higher Education, the completion of which gave professional registration status. Developing regional links with the NHS, and working with the nearby Sefton School of Health Studies, the College drafted a proposal which was eventually accepted as the first such programme in the North West, with the

*The campus of the Sefton School of Health Studies at Fazakerley Hospital, Aintree (shown above) was the base for most of the School's work.*

initial intake of Nursing students commencing their studies in September 1990 (corresponding provision for Midwifery commenced in 1993). Most of the teaching took place at the existing premises of the Sefton School of Health Studies at Fazakerley Hospital in Aintree, and some additional demountable accommodation was provided at Ormskirk. The College now offered academic provision leading to professional status for two major professions, a pattern which was to be repeated many times over the years. Governors realised the longer-term potential of this development and in 1991 agreed in principle that the Sefton School of Health Studies should be 'assimilated' into the College at a 'mutually agreed date': the merger eventually took place in two phases in 1993 and 1994.

The incorporation of the School of Health Studies was an important stage in the history of Edge Hill. The College was now responsible for the education and training of professionals in two major sectors, and the wider influence of the institution had a strong Merseyside focus, which was to be important in the years to come.

### Academic Infrastructure

Alongside these curriculum developments, Gee set out to build a new academic management infrastructure. Four members of the senior team had indicated their intention to retire in summer 1991, and this presented opportunities for academic restructuring. At incorporation, academic provision was based around three faculties (Initial Teacher Education, INSET, and Humanities, Environmental and Social Sciences). Early in 1991, the Deans of Initial Teacher Education and INSET proposed that the two Faculties should merge into a single Faculty of Teacher Education. This proposal was accepted, but the longer-term position of the 25 (mostly small) academic areas within the third faculty was not to be resolved until 1993.

Gee recognised that the College needed to develop academic frameworks and structures on the lines of those in the successful polytechnics and larger colleges of higher education. Quality assurance processes were, at that time, underdeveloped compared with those in the majority of the PCFC sector, but the first Quality Assurance handbook, in the form of the *Procedures for course approval, validation, monitoring and review* was published in 1991. The Procedures adopted an important and fundamental principle that '...Peer review is an essential element in maintaining and improving standards, and the procedures are designed to make use of a wide range of expertise, both internal and external to the college'. Although the external peer element was mainly restricted to Lancaster University up to 1993, the Procedures represented an important building block for the College.

The Modularisation Working Group, working in 1990 and 1991, was constructing another such block. As provision outside teacher education in the humanities, social and applied sciences was growing, the merits

*The dated 1980s computer infrastructure was replaced in the early 1990s.*

of developing a modular degree scheme, affording greater levels of student choice, were becoming recognised. These were common (but by no means universal) in the polytechnics and colleges, encouraged by the CNAA's Credit Accumulation and Transfer Scheme of 1986, but rare at that time in the university sector. The Working Group proposed to the Academic Board the establishment of a modular BA/BSc degree scheme, with provision for credit accumulation and transfer. The scheme built on the existing Lancaster University undergraduate model, with the intention of developing single honours, major-minor and joint honours routes in the future. The proposal, approved by the Academic Board in June 1991, took some years to develop to its full potential under the leadership of Dr (later Professor) Brian Maidment as Dean of Modular Programmes, but it remains, in a recognisable form, the basis of all undergraduate provision across the University to this day.

### Teaching and Learning

Gee realised that if the College was to fulfil its ambitions, expressed in the Strategic Plan, to provide 'excellent teaching', effective institutional leadership would be required. In 1992, Dr (later Emeritus Professor) Andrew Sackville was appointed to the new post of Head of Teaching and Learning Development. This was an important and radical step as, at that time, relatively few institutions had a senior postholder with equivalent responsibilities. Sackville had already developed short, in-house courses on Teaching and Learning in Higher Education, and his enthusiastic and committed approach ensured the development of the College's first Teaching and Learning Strategy in 1994.

The lack of any significant IT infrastructure in support of teaching and learning was apparent: in the late 1980s there were a small number of PCs and Macintoshes and some enthusiasts in individual departments, but no institution-wide approach to

*A geography field trip to Newcastle in the 1980s. John Cater (fourth from the left) can be seen listening intently.*

IT investment. A decision was made in 1990 that every student and member of staff was to have an IT entitlement: 'No matter what course a student is following, IT should be a formal part of everyday learning. Every student should have an entitlement to develop a practical capability in IT which is more than a mere knowledge of extant systems.' In 1993 a million-pound partnership deal was made with the (then) leading computer manufacturer ICL for the provision of networked computers for staff and students. The College was starting its journey towards what was to become, 15 years later, a national Centre of Excellence in Teaching and Learning.

## Research

The low research profile of the College at the time has already been noted. With a handful of exceptions (most notably Phil Scraton in Criminology and Don Moyle in the Teaching of Reading), academic staff engaged successfully in advanced scholarship but were not required, or in some areas even encouraged, to engage in research. The College described itself in the 1991 Strategic Plan as 'primarily a teaching and learning institution'. A decision had been taken not to enter the College in the first national Research Assessment Exercise (RAE) for which it was eligible, in 1992: since almost all polytechnics and many colleges chose to enter at this time, this was seen by some as a retrograde step.

Nevertheless, some important developments were undertaken. The Research Committee, which had been established in the 1980s, was raising the profile of research across the College, and a proposal to appoint personal professorships was agreed by the Academic Board and the Board of Governors in 1990. Soon after, Moyle and Scraton became the first colleagues to receive this award. For some years in the early 1990s, Scraton's Centre for Studies in Crime and Social Justice (CSCSJ) was the most active research centre in the College and contributed much to the raising of the institution's profile in the wider academic community. The first students registered on MPhil/PhD programmes started their study. Alongside this, research activity in English, History, Social Sciences and Geography was enhanced. Research across the university, however, lacked an overall focus and strategic direction.

## Student Support

An important aspect of the College's infrastructure that required enhancement was that of student support. In 1991 Sue Aldridge was appointed Head of Student Services, a new senior management post, to provide a comprehensive student services support structure. This was a vast undertaking involving not just student discipline and halls management but also accommodation, child care, counselling and student health services. A three-year development plan was produced to initiate the desired changes. It was felt that the existing system of Hall Wardens and Hall Presidents worked against equal opportunities and promoted some of the worst features of a public school ethos. Wardens became Residential Advisors who worked alongside Student Assistants who were fully trained in equal opportunities and in mediation and conflict resolution.

***Joe Ainsworth, BA English and Communications 1986–89***

Joe Ainsworth is a BAFTA winning screenwriter working on well-known TV productions such as *Holby City*, *A&E*, *Brookside*, *Merseybeat* and *The Lakes*.

He graduated in 1989 with a degree in English and Communications and began writing professionally following a chance meeting with famous Liverpool writer Jimmy McGovern. After showing him some sample work Joe was offered a trial writing stint on Channel 4 soap opera *Brookside*, impressing executive producer Phil Redmond to be taken on as a permanent member of the writing team. He returned to work with McGovern on *The Lakes II* and one of his most rewarding projects – his own eight-part series, *And the Beat Goes On*, which was set in Liverpool in the sixties. He currently works on *Holby City* and is about to start work on new BBC drama *No Man's Land*.

**Access and Equal Opportunities**

While Gee had inherited a Strategic Plan for 1989–92 from the previous management, this required significant development, and a revised Strategic Plan to 1993 was submitted to PCFC in June 1990. For the first time, the College had a (now *de rigueur*) Mission Statement, committing the institution to 'provide a stimulating learning environment which develops transferable expertise and skills necessary for the worlds of work and leisure' and to 'offer flexible access and opportunity to members of under-represented groups'. This latter statement signalled what was to become a major strand of college activity as widening participation became a major government and council priority, starting with the 1990 PCFC paper *Widening Participation in Higher Education*. Edge Hill entered into a partnership with its nearest further education college, Skelmersdale College, through which students were able to study for the first year of a three-year honours degree in a range of disciplines in Skelmersdale, transferring to Edge Hill for their second and third years of study.

A similar project was initiated with Wirral Metropolitan College, through which students studied a one-year access 'year zero' programme, which for funding purposes was treated as the first year of an integrated four-year honours degree programme. On completion of 'year zero' students transferred to Ormskirk for the remainder of their studies: this became a model for other similar programmes undertaken in partnership with the open college networks in the 1990s.

Despite the fact that Edge Hill had begun life as a Women's Training College, its management by the 1980s had taken on a distinctively masculine face. Miranda Bell was appointed as a member of the Directorate in 1990, and through her an Access and Equal Opportunities Unit was established, exemplifying a new commitment to equal opportunities for both students and staff. An Equal Opportunities policy was developed, covering all aspects of the life of the College. There was no doubt that the ideas of equal opportunities permeating all aspects took time, particularly with regard to course content. Nevertheless the policy was an important aspect of attempts to create a quality culture stressing the values of honesty, trust, respect and empowerment.

In this connection, the APTAB (Access to Primary Teaching for Asian and Black People) project was developed in the early 1990s between Edge Hill College, S Martin's College, Lancaster University and Lancashire County Council. The project aimed to bring more people from black and ethnic groups into teaching: at the time there were only seven such out of 5,000 primary teachers in Lancashire. Students took the first part of their degree in local colleges in East and Central Lancashire, alongside professional work at a Professional Centre in Blackburn, attending Edge Hill for aspects of their work in later years. Although programme numbers were never high, much was learnt from the project that was to be of value as the College developed its partnership and collaborative work in later years.

### College Administration

In the early 1990s, the College was not well known outside its local area. Most undergraduate applicants came from the North West region, and, despite 15 years of diversification, Edge Hill was seen by most as still a teacher training college. Many senior staff in the education world outside the region would struggle to locate Edge Hill to within 100 miles. Some visitors, travelling to the College, would alight at Edge Hill station in Liverpool, close to the institution's original location, only realising their error on phoning the College to establish its location. Accordingly, a new Marketing unit was established, initially with two staff. Alongside this there was the development of professional support in Personnel (later Human Resources). Following some criticism in the external auditor's report relating the first annual financial statement in 1990, there was some much-needed investment in staffing and in IT systems.

*The 'semester abroad' programme, started in 1990, continues to provide American students with a valuable academic and social experience.*

### The International Dimension

As 1992 and the creation of the Single European Market grew nearer, the importance of developing a broader curriculum and links with continental Europe were recognised. Under Colin Pickthall (soon to be elected Labour Member of Parliament for West Lancashire) a new undergraduate degree in Modern European Studies was developed in 1991, along with a combined French and English degree. At the same time, a paper entitled 'Developing links with Europe' was approved by the Academic Board. Through the Faculty of Teacher Education, links were developed with Universität Osnabruck and the Weingarten Pedagogisches Hochschule in Germany.

This was part of a growing international strand of activity within the institution: the College's new commercial company, Edge Hill Enterprises, developed links in the United States with a number of partner universities and colleges, and the first intake of 20 American undergraduates joined the College in September 1990 for their 'semester abroad' programme, a venture which continues to the present day. The President of Baldwin-Wallace College in Ohio visited Edge Hill in December 1990 and administered the Educator's Oath of the State of Ohio, the first time that such an oath had been administered outside the US.

### The Ormskirk Estate

In 1989 the imposing facade of the main building as seen from St Helens Road gave a false impression. The lack of investment in teaching, learning and other facilities for students in the past 20 years had to be addressed as a matter of urgency. With low reserves, and only small surpluses being developed, this presented a challenge: Gee noted in her first report to Governors that 'Finance for capital and minor building works would be urgently needed if the planned growth in student numbers were to be adequately catered for'.

During 1991 and 1992 a series of campus improvements were undertaken. The front entrance to the main building was modified and extended to allow disabled access, although the new, green, arched entrance structure was not admired by all. The dowdy teaching accommodation on the first floor 'M' corridor of the main building was refurbished and provided with modern audio-visual facilities, while a new lift to the first floor ensured access for all to these resources.

As student numbers had risen, the 1971 library had become too small and the collection was split between

*The main building, painted by Chris Millichamp, showing the new entrance completed in 1992. The sculptures by Robert Scriven, from a series called 'Life Games', were installed in 1989.*

The new Learning Resources Centre (LRC), built in 1993/4.

two buildings, with the 'Education Resource Centre' located in the original college dining room. In 1992 the PCFC invited bids for the development of estates, and the College was awarded £1.13m towards the total cost of £2.8m for the construction of a new Learning Resources Centre (LRC), designed by the Liverpool architects Weightman and Bullen.

Bob Wilson (Chair of Governors at the time) commented:

> *There was serious concern on the part of Governors about the condition of the estate, the provision for students and the needs of teaching staff. We were certainly behind other institutions in facilities and maintenance, and behind the times in technological terms.*
>
> *The first real breakthrough, from the Governors' point of view, was the success in the bid to the funding council for a Learning Resource Centre, and the ability to borrow for the construction of the new Forest Court student accommodation. Our bankers were kind in lending us 100 per cent of the cost against the security of the final building. Calculations showed that it would pay for itself without any contribution from the normal College income.*

A new period of major investment in the Ormskirk Campus therefore started in 1993 with the construction of the LRC, the foundation stone of which was laid in early 1993 by Tim Boswell, Minister for Further and Higher Education. The 4,500m² LRC was completed in

Above: The Forest Court student accommodation building.

late 1993, and formally opened by Professor Graeme Davies, Chief Executive of HEFCE (Higher Education Funding Council for England) in early 1994, who paid tribute to Edge Hill's 'obvious commitment to excellence in higher education', noting the 'star quality' of its staff and students. Its carefully considered design, under a team led by the Head of Library Services Ruth Jenkinson, has stood the test of time. The 250,000 books, periodicals and multimedia collections were supplemented by over 150 open access PCs for student use, and the internal layout allowed ample facilities for group study areas, quiet study areas and individual study carrels. Through its integration of facilities for student learning needs, the LRC design was, at the time, 'state of the art', and influenced other similar university and college developments that followed across the country. Ruth Jenkinson comments:

> *A series of major changes were required of the staff working in the new LRC. Some were nervous of the sheer size and scale of the building – especially in the evenings and weekends when there were fewer staff on duty. Library staff working closely alongside computing staff at that time was still relatively unusual in the sector and there was a considerable process involved in understanding the cultural differences and learning to work together as a cohesive and client-facing team. Restructuring of the library service was a vital development, which was not without its controversy as staff saw the 'old order' disappear and much more demanding progressive skills and flexibility requirements grow. Many staff also developed additional self-confidence and perhaps greater personal ambition, as the former 'Cinderella syndrome' which in the past tended to afflict library staff, who were sometimes seen as worthy and committed individuals but somewhat lacking in personal impact and professional standing, was well and truly challenged.*

In 1993, planning had started for new £3.25m student residential accommodation: Forest Court was to comprise over 300 high-quality study bedrooms with computer network access, and two rooms specially designed for the needs of disabled students.

The new visual identity designed in 1992 to recognise Edge Hill's 'University Sector College' title.

Edge Hill
a
UNIVERSITY
sector
COLLEGE

### Accreditation, 'University College' title and the Binary Line

In 1991 the first of a long period of discussions on the College title commenced. The Director noted a concern about the profile of colleges of HE. The formal designation as a 'College of Higher Education' was clumsy, and the institution wished to find means to differentiate itself from further education colleges, preferably by adopting the 'university college' title. At that time, there were only two types of institution that could formally adopt this title: those that were an integrated component of an existing university or those that were formally 'accredited' by their validating body. Governors noted in March 1991 that 39 out of 85 PCFC institutions already had accredited status (mostly through the CNAA). Accordingly, discussions on the accreditation process started with Lancaster University, with a series of panel visits taking place in 1992. In the meantime, the College neatly and accurately described its position through a new visual identity describing itself as 'a university sector college'.

However the HE sector was now shaken by another major policy change. The 1991 White Paper *HE – A New Framework* had signalled what was described at the time as the 'ending of the binary line' through the re-designation of the polytechnics and some other 'major institutions' as universities. The two funding councils, PCFC and UFC, were to be merged into a single Higher Education Funding Council for England (HEFCE), with parallel bodies in Scotland and Wales. Since the newly created universities (or 'post 1992' universities, as they quickly became known) were to have the same powers as those in the existing university sector, they would have their own powers to award both taught and research degrees, regardless of whether they had any experience in the latter field (this was a bitter pill for the College to swallow years later when it fought long and hard for its own research degree-awarding powers). The CNAA was to be 'laid down' and sector-wide scrutiny of institutional quality assurance arrangements would be transferred to a new body, the Higher Education Quality Council (HEQC), owned by the HE sector but strongly influenced by government policies and demands. HEFCE would undertake the quality assessment of teaching across all subjects in the HE sector in England. The Further and Higher Education Act of 1992 approved the changes and, within months, all of the polytechnics (including, in the North West region, those in Manchester, Liverpool and Preston), along with a handful of larger colleges of HE with CNAA accredited status, had adopted new university titles.

Gee's paper for Governors in July 1991 stated that '...colleges of HE are potentially quite vulnerable as freestanding institutions within a new broader HE sector without a binary line'. In reality, from the perspective of Edge Hill and the remaining HE colleges, the binary line had not been removed but shifted. The number of universities had more than doubled and the remaining 52 colleges of higher education comprised a diverse group in terms of size, breadth of portfolio and academic and financial viability: half of these institutions were to change or lose their identity through merger or closure as independent entities over the next ten years.

Another blow to the College came in 1992 with the first HMI inspection for some years, and the first to review the developing provision, outside Initial Teacher Training (ITT), in the humanities and sciences. Provision in English was regarded at 'satisfactory with good features', Biology was 'satisfactory' and History and Geography were judged to be 'unsatisfactory'. Aspects of cross-college student support, including levels of IT provision, were strongly criticised. While the parallel inspection of Initial Teacher Training judged provision in that area to be 'excellent', the overall findings, for a college that had prided itself on its teaching and student support, were both salutary and devastating.

*Edge Hill opened its sculpture park in 1989. Opposite: the latest sculpture to be installed on campus is 'Goat' by Tony Evans. It was commissioned as part of the University's 125th anniversary celebrations.*

### Ruth Gee's Achievements

By 1993, Gee's relationship with the Board of Governors was deteriorating. The past two years had seen the College finances running at a loss, despite an increase in student numbers, with deficits that were small but not sustainable beyond the short term. The HMI inspection of 1992 had exposed significant underlying academic problems. While the academic portfolio outside Initial Teacher Training had begun to grow, the ITT portfolio itself was still very limited.

Gee, however, had many achievements to show. She had provided strong, brave and committed leadership through the difficult post-incorporation period, had started to modernise many aspects of the College's management structures and academic infrastructure, and had initiated a long period of culture change across the College, challenging a culture of complacency. Student numbers had grown and the redevelopment of the estate had started.Gee had a regular column in the *Times Higher Education Supplement* that succeeded in raising the profile of the College in the wider higher education community. The College was much stronger in 1993 than it had been in 1989. However, in the summer of that year she resigned from the College to take up the post of Director of the newly formed Association of Colleges.

# John Cater Takes Over

6

## A New Director and Management Team

John Cater had already worked at Edge Hill for 14 years prior to his appointment as Director. A geographer by training, he had a doctorate from Liverpool Polytechnic in *Immigration, Segregation and the Development of Asian Retail and Service Business*. As a lecturer and senior lecturer in the Geography department, he had played a leading role in the development of the subject in the College, and had led the successful Urban Policy and Race Relations (UPRR) programme in the 1980s. At that time he also co-wrote a successful university textbook on social geography and published widely on public policy matters. He had moved through a senior faculty position to the institutional posts of Head of Policy, Planning and Development and then to Director of Resources. His knowledge of the planning process, of Liverpool politics and of local NHS structures (through his involvement in the development of the successful Project 2000 Nursing bid in the late 1980s) were all to prove to be invaluable in the years to follow. Following his appointment, and through the College's membership of the Standing Conference of Principals (SCoP) he was appointed as Chair of the SCoP Teacher Education Group in 1995 and to SCoP Board membership in 1996.

In 1992, Mark Flinn had joined Edge Hill as Director of Academic Affairs and Quality Management, bringing with him experience from the former Council for National Academic Awards (CNAA) institutions, Buckinghamshire College of Higher Education and Thames Valley University. Early in 1994, Rhiannon Evans (later awarded a professorial title) was appointed to the post of Director of Students and External Relations: her experience in the further education sector was to prove invaluable as the College sought to develop its widening participation mission and its partnership work. Steve Igoe, formerly with Coopers, Lybrand and Deloitte (now PricewaterhouseCoopers) joined the College as Head of Finance and Resources in January 1996 and was promoted to the post of Director of Resources in 1997. The four Directorate members Cater, Evans, Flinn and Igoe were to work together on the Directorate team for more than ten years in what was to be among the most significant periods of the institution's history.

*Mark Flinn (left) became Director of Academic Affairs and Quality Management in 1992 and Steve Igoe became Head of Finance and Resources in 1996.*

The revised Mission Statement pledged that the College would:

John Cater.

*Build on people, by using and developing our skills to enhance the learning process and add value to the experience of students from a wide range of backgrounds through a variety of routes.*
*Build on location, by strengthening our ties with the local community through vocational work and collaborative networks.*
*Build for quality, by continuing to develop and strengthen the range and delivery of our academic programmes.*

### Institutional Title and Status

The position of the College in 1993 on the wrong side of the newly-drawn binary line was noted in the previous chapter. Ensuring accreditation from Lancaster University, eventually achieved in September 1994, was a first step in moving towards achieving greater levels of academic autonomy. The validation model (the process through which new academic provision is formally approved at institutional level) was developed so that it more closely resembled that at the former CNAA institutions. Most significantly, the validation events took place at Edge Hill rather than culminating in the meetings of the relevant Lancaster University committee. The adoption of the principles of peer review within the College took time to become established: in the early days, some colleagues thought it 'unprofessional' to question the work of others within the institution. Gradually, however, over a period of years, an appropriate and self-critical model of internal peer review evolved.

With the formal granting of accredited status, and with written support from Lancaster University, the College was now free legitimately to adopt the 'University College' title, which it duly did in January

1996. The former 'University Sector' style was replaced by a new corporate identity and the title of Edge Hill University College. This was, however, not to last for long.

In the same academic year, a document *Towards a Regional University* was developed and widely circulated among stakeholders and the community. This document, for the first time, publically signalled Edge Hill's ambitions, which were to take ten years to come to fruition.

### Developing and Diversifying the Academic Portfolio

By September 1993, the academic work of the College had been organised into five Schools. The School of Education and the School of Health Studies (which formally merged with the College early in 1994) were supplemented by the three new Schools of Humanities & Arts, Management & Social Sciences, and Sciences & Technology. These three Schools were responsible for the work of what was then known as the modular scheme, along with 'subject study' on Primary and the (now quickly developing) Secondary Initial Teacher Training (ITT) provision.

The other significant factor that was to influence the development of the three 'new' Schools was the size of the component academic departments. With over 20 departments (some comprising only a handful of academic staff) across the three Schools, the smallest lacked the critical mass of staff to create a viable university level department. The process of 'rationalisation' of departments, through merger, transfer to the School of Education or (on occasions) closure was to be another major thread of institutional change in the 1990s.

In the growth period of the 1990s, the five Schools proved to be strong engines of curriculum development. New programmes in the new Schools followed: Women's Studies, Creative Writing, Art and Drama in Humanities & Arts; Leisure Management, Critical Criminology, Disability & Community Studies and Marketing in Management & Social Sciences; and Information Systems and Sports Studies in Sciences & Technology. All of the undergraduate provision in these three Schools was within the Modular Scheme, which by 1997 had accommodated over 200 study combinations (single honours, major/minor and joint honours routes).

In the School of Education, secondary Initial Teacher Training (ITT) provision continued its expansion with support from the new Teacher Training Agency, with the PGCE English, Design Technology and Business Education being supplemented by Science and Mathematics (1993) and Modern Foreign Languages (1994). By 1997, these had been followed by History, Geography, Information Technology and Physical Education. The two-year 'shortened' BSc secondary QTS courses were converted to three-year honours degree programmes, helping to ensure their long-term future.

In the area of Primary ITT, the publication by the Department of Education and Science (DES) of Circular 14/93 'The Initial Training of Primary School Teachers: New Criteria for Courses' signalled major changes in the Primary ITT curriculum, following the abolition of the Council for the Accreditation of Teacher Education (CATE), by reducing the proportion of 'subject study' within the four-year BA/BSc (QTS) programme. The consequential impact on the small departments elsewhere in the College providing subject study took time to unravel. Meanwhile, partnerships with schools continued to grow: in 1993 the College had working relationships with 471 primary schools, 56 secondary schools and 15 further education colleges.

The middle period in the decade saw three important developments, which were to have major impacts on the development of the School of Education. In 1995, through what became a major element of ITT provision over the next ten years, the first 'Middle Years' programme in English was launched, initially at PGCE level: the programme qualified graduates to teach in the upper years of primary schools and the lower years of secondary schools. Secondly, through a partnership with the Borough of Wigan, a successful Primary Articled Teacher scheme was developed, initially with 30 students, and the experience gained from the project was invaluable as further 'non-traditional' routes

*Secondary Initial Teacher Training (ITT) continued to expand in the 1990s, with the Middle Years programme, the Primary Articled Teacher scheme, and the Specialist Teacher Assistants (STA) programme.*

into teaching were developed by the TTA later in the decade. Finally, a new programme for 'Specialist Teacher Assistants' (STA), supported by Lancashire County Council, was developed and successfully operated from 1995. Five years later, when foundation degrees (FDs) were launched, the experience gained through the STA programme was invaluable in ensuring a successful bid to HEFCE for additional student numbers to support a new FD for Classroom Assistants. The foundations for future diversification in the School of Education were being laid.

The School of Health Studies, following its formal merger and incorporation with the College in 1994, undertook its academic development, initially at a slower rate. There were two principal contributing factors here: the main location of the School at Fazakerley Hospital in Aintree, 12 miles away from Ormskirk, militated against regular interaction between academics in the School and those based at Ormskirk, and so opportunities for collaboration between the School of Health Studies and the Ormskirk-based schools were limited. Secondly, the School was dependent at that time on commissions from the Regional Health Authority for student numbers and new provision, and these commissions were hard for a non-university institution to achieve, at least up to the later years of the decade. The pre-registration diploma provision in Nursing and Midwifery, alongside a small but growing range of post-experience modules and programmes contributing to the English National Board (ENB) Higher Award, formed the bulk of the School's work. A well-developed link with the Liverpool Marie Curie Centre formed the basis for an innovative programme in Cancer Care. As a signal of its commitment to staff development, the School gained 'Investors in People' status in 1996, prompting the College to prepare its own successful application in the following year.

### External Academic Scrutiny

Prior to the 1990s, the extent of external scrutiny of academic provision was limited to occasional HMI inspections. All of this was to change following the 1993 Further and Higher Education Act.

HMI became part of the new Office for Standards in Education (Ofsted), and an intensive period of regular inspections by teams comprising HMI and trained inspectors visited the College most years, to inspect aspects of ITT and INSET provision. The inspection of 1993 assessed Primary ITT provision as good (and excellent in parts), with Secondary provision being regarded as excellent throughout. Most inspections of the rapidly developing Secondary provision yielded good or excellent outcomes, but the Primary 'sweep' inspection of 1996, while judging the provision in three areas to be 'good', found the provision in English only 'satisfactory', an outcome that was confirmed on re-inspection the following year. Inspection outcomes were linked to the numbers of funded places and there was a resultant long-term impact on Primary funded student numbers.

The second major change, resulting from the Further and Higher Education Act, was the establishment of 'Teaching Quality Assessment' (TQA) of all provision in HE outside teacher education. Up to 1998 this was initially undertaken directly by HEFCE through its Quality Assessment Division, on a subject-by-subject basis. The first rounds in 1993 and 1994 confirmed provision in Management, English, History and Geography as 'satisfactory', while in January 1995 the provision in Social Sciences and Criminology was assessed as 'excellent'. Assessors commented on the high-quality teaching, accommodation and learning resources. HEFCE also used the 1993 Ofsted evidence to confirm provision in Secondary ITT as 'excellent': the College became one of only four HEIs (Higher Education Institutes) in the country in this category.

The HEFCE methodology changed in 1995–6 with the publication of a profile of grades in six 'aspects' of provision, with each aspect being graded between 4 (excellent) and 1 (unsatisfactory). Unofficially, but to the delight of league table providers, scores could be aggregated to a total out of the maximum possible of 24: a threshold score of 22 was commonly regarded as representing excellent provision. Under this methodology up to 1997, the small provision in French was graded 18/24, Media 20/24, Urban Policy Studies 17/24 and Drama a disappointing 14/24. These results were disappointing by any standard.

The final academic review process from 1993 was the introduction of 'Academic Audit', administered by the new Higher Education Quality Council (HEQC). This process focused on quality assurance processes at institutional level rather than within individual disciplines or departments. Edge Hill's first such audit was held in 1996: with no summative grades, the final audit report was not written for a lay audience and required some decoding, but it was generally agreed that it provided a sound foundation for a bid for the newly defined taught degree-awarding powers (TDAP). By this stage, HEQC and the Department for Education had determined that in order to become a university, institutions, alongside meeting threshold criteria on size and breadth of provision, would have to have gained both TDAP and research degree-awarding powers (RDAP). While the former appeared at that time within sight, the latter was a very tall order for an institution with a limited research profile and (at that time) a small number of doctoral students.

The twin systems of TQA through HEFCE and academic audit through HEQC, with different and sometimes conflicting cultures and requirements, were heavily criticised by universities and colleges. In 1997, the DES supported the principle that both the processes should be run by the same agency, and, closing the HEQC, created the new Quality Assurance Agency (QAA) under its combative Chief Executive, John Randall, to do this.

### Research and Consultancy

The mid-1990s saw the start of the period when research was undertaken more strategically at Edge Hill. In 1993, the College had invested in a series of research student scholarships, and by 1995 there were a dozen full-time doctoral students across the College, the majority in the three 'new' Schools, along with a growing number of part-time students. 1995–6 saw the first PhD graduate, with Edward Whall's thesis *Back to the Bridewell: Punishment and Police Custody 1980-1994*. The increasing volume of research students necessitated the formation, with the support of Lancaster University, of the Research Degrees Committee, responsible for monitoring the progression of research students and approving their examination arrangements.

Professor Phil Scraton's Centre for Studies in Crime and Social Justice (CSCSJ) remained pre-eminent and influential within and outside the College: his book on the 1989 Hillsborough Disaster was published in 1995. But other new centres were formed: In the School of Health Studies, the Centre for Health Research and Evaluation (CHRE) was established under its Director, Dr (later Professor) Tom Chapman. The Centre undertook several large research projects for local NHS trusts, including a study of the health and social care of the Formby elderly, undertaken jointly with Alan Johnson (awarded a Professorial title ten years later) from the Department of Applied Social Sciences.

In the same department, the Centre for Local Policy Studies (CLPS), established by Dr (later Professor) John Diamond and Stuart Speeden in 1994, started its successful development as a centre for knowledge transfer and research into equalities, youth issues and other local government priorities.

The College had not entered the first Research Assessment Exercise (RAE) for which it was eligible in 1992. It did however, enter the next RAE in 1996, and achieved creditable grades in four areas, each of which demonstrated research of national excellence: English, History, Social Sciences and Education. This outcome was to generate funding of over £200,000 a year for the next five years, placing the College as the best first entrant in the *Times Higher Education Supplement* research league table.

### Information Technology: The Rise of the World Wide Web

By the mid-1990s the College's investment in IT was starting to bear fruit, following the development of the College's first Information strategy. The LRC was packed with computers and, from then on, every new building would incorporate computer suites. Up to this time, computers were mainly used by students for standard application packages (word processing, email, spreadsheets) and for using the LRC's large collection of CD-roms. The rise of the World Wide Web changed this completely. In 1993 around 50 staff had access to the web. Two years later all staff had access: the links of the College to the Joint Academic Network (JANET) were significantly enhanced through SuperJANET in 1995 as the College had access to what then were considered high-speed networks. Andrew Sackville, Head of Teaching and Learning Development, working with colleagues across the university, started to develop a community of practice that was to pay dividends to the institution in the future.

In 1995 Edge Hill's first website was launched. The Annual Report 1994/95 commented: 'Edge Hill opened its virtual doors to around 25 million people when it launched its first live home page on the World Wide Web. Edgeweb went online early in 1995, with spin-off pages linking to the local newspaper, community events and other academic sites. Interest generated by the pages was widespread.' The same report noted a major multimedia project investigating the potential of CD-roms in student recruitment: the resulting

The Student Information Centre (SIC) was set up in the old Library building in 1994.

StudyLink CD-rom was launched in May 1995 with a wide distribution to schools and colleges. In response to these and other changes in the learning environment, the College pioneered one of the first postgraduate certificates in Teaching and Learning in Higher Education in 1995.

The College's administrative systems responded to the technological changes. A new and more robust student record system, HEMIS, was introduced and email communication started to become an everyday, even pervasive, part of College life.

### Student Support

The completion of the LRC in 1994 freed the former 1971 Library building for alternative uses. Up to this date, services supporting students had been located in different buildings across the Ormskirk campus. It was agreed to relocate Student Systems and Administration, the Office of Modular Programmes, Student Services and the Careers Office as a 'one-stop shop' in the old Library building, now entitled the Student Information Centre (SIC). A key feature of the SIC was the single helpdesk, which provided a range of advice for students and referred them, where appropriate, to the specialist services within the building: by the end of its first year, the helpdesk was handling over 400 queries per week.

This model of integrated student support was an early example of what is now universal in higher education. The 1996 HEQC Audit report noted '...the team would wish to commend the particularly active approach of the Library, Student Services and Careers Services in supporting students'. The SIC has remained to the present day as a very tangible sign of the institution's commitment to integrated student support and guidance.

The importance of providing new undergraduate students with a formal induction programme had been recognised. In 1994, new first-year students

joined the seven-day 'Firstweek' programme, which provided a carefully managed blend of induction to college facilities and support, an introduction to academic study and degree-level study skills, and a structured social element which went beyond the pub crawls of the 1980s. Firstweek was subject to a detailed evaluation (friendliness, facilities and student support networks all scored highly in the first survey) and, although it has changed over the years, its founding principles have stood the test of time.

Empowering students to become active members of the College community was important for the institution's development. This was the principle behind the Students' Charter, devised in 1995 after detailed consultation with the Students' Union and other representatives. Along with the formulation of a new complaints procedure, the Charter marked a new era of partnership between Edge Hill and its students. It set out the standards that the College would strive to achieve for all students, intending students, employers and the local community. For each year since then, the College has undertaken a survey of student satisfaction (anticipating the national surveys which were to start ten years later), which has guided the development of services and support for students.

In 1996, HEFCE awarded the College £164,000 for the support of disabled students. With the new Disability and Community Studies degree programme now recruiting students, Edge Hill was establishing itself as a leader in this area.

## Widening Participation and Partnerships

The period of the mid-1990s saw an increasing government commitment to widening participation. The College was well placed to develop initiatives in this area with its links with secondary schools and further education colleges, and its proximity to areas of historically low participation in higher education.

***Peter Davies, Bachelor of Education 1969–73***

Peter Davies is a legal consultant for the European Commission on Internet safety, rubbing shoulders with the likes of Mikhail Gorbachev and Bill Gates in a colourful career journey that started at Edge Hill University. Originally qualifying as a teacher, he took a post at a boys' grammar school in Southport, lasting just 12 months before deciding teaching wasn't his vocation. At the age of 29 he undertook a postgraduate diploma in Law and entered the legal profession, quickly rising to the top with posts in a number of high profile companies. He was the first lawyer to be hired by Microsoft outside the US, and worked as Head of Law for the Software Division of IBM, before joining Apple as European Legal Director.

In 1995 the College was one of only 47 institutions to be supported by the first HEFCE Widened Provision Fund, and was awarded one of the largest grants. Through this support, the College developed its Widening Access strategy. 'Aiming for a College Education' (ACE) days were targeted at year 9–11 schoolchildren in the region, and were designed to raise awareness of higher education among groups of young people from families and communities without previous experience of higher education. Edge Hill joined the Liverpool HiPACT (Higher Education Compact), jointly funded by the European Social Fund and Liverpool City Council, which undertook a range of awareness-raising activities with school pupils from backgrounds with no tradition of participation in higher education. Edge Hill also joined the Liverpool City of Learning project and through that contributed to the economic regeneration of the city. Collaborative arrangements were extended with Halton College, Wigan and Leigh College, Skelmersdale College, Southport College and St Helens College. Blackburn College became the principal centre for the previously mentioned APTAB 'Lancashire Project'.

In the meantime, the College was enhancing its links with the Open College Networks (OCNs) in the region: its long-term active participation in the Regional and Merseyside Networks was supplemented by membership of the Manchester Open College Network. Access provision was booming, and the College felt there was a need for a short, intensive access programme for mature students to supplement the one-year access courses run through the OCNs. The College won further grants from HEFCE, and 1997 saw the launch of Edge Hill's first access programme, Fastrack: an intensive six-week (later seven-week) programme of study designed for adults with few or no academic qualifications but with the ability to benefit from higher education. There were no entry qualifications other than motivation and the desire to succeed. The first Fastrack cohort had 12 students: the 2009 cohort had 234 students: several Fastrack students have gone on to achieve first-class honours degrees.

*The early 1990s saw developments in student life with construction of the Venue, the Terrace Café and a new Students' Union.*

## Edge Hill Enterprises

The College commercial company, Edge Hill Enterprises (EHE), whose initial activities had focused on the recruitment of visiting US semester students, developed its commercial work significantly during the mid-1990s: by 1994 its annual turnover was £1.6m, reaching £4.5m two years later. The substantial surpluses generated by EHE during this period were not used to subsidise the College's revenue budget: they were used only for capital investment.

EHE commenced work as an NVQ assessment centre and won over £300,000 from the European Social Fund towards its Merseyside-based training provision. To support these training programmes, a new Vocational Training Centre was built adjacent to the School of Health Studies building in Aintree, opening in December 1996, and a new Business Cyber Centre was opened in Skelmersdale, providing modern IT facilities and training packages, and a growing range of English Language summer schools was run.

## Development of the Estate

The construction of the LRC and Forest Court in the early 1990s was the start of a period of investment in the Ormskirk estate and infrastructure that has continued to this day. Student facilities were the first priority: the Students' Union was moved from its base in the main building and relocated, with an adjoining social centre, 'the Venue', alongside the shop, a new fast-food outlet and the college bar. The vacated space in the main building was rebuilt to form the 'Terrace Cafe', centrally located by the main internal courtyard. The former Education Resources Centre accommodation was converted to allow the restoration of the fine 1933 college dining room to something approaching its original state.

Edge Hill was determined to develop a broad curriculum that would include applied and environmental sciences. The dated facilities in the old 'Arts and Science' building required enhancement as the College's science provision developed: in addition to the established Primary Science subject study of the

*A new rugby pitch and running track were built on the eastern end of campus in the early 1990s.*

1980s the College now offered Secondary BSc QTS and PGCE Science courses alongside the small but successful BSc Field Biology and Habitat Management. A new building was required, and the Natural and Applied Sciences building was opened in 1995 towards the rear of the campus. Nearby, a single-storey extension was added to the 'Levens' building to accommodate the growing ITT Mathematics provision.

Another major priority was the enhancement of the Sports facilities. In the early 1990s these comprised a rugby pitch and running track towards the eastern end of the campus, a gymnasium in the centre of the campus (supplemented by a physical education laboratory in 1995) and playing fields at the western end of the campus. While adequate for a diversifying teacher training college, significant investment was necessary to provide modern facilities for the developing Sports Studies and Physical Education provision, as well as leisure facilities for students. With this in mind, 25 acres of land on the eastern end of the campus were leased in 1995 for 300 years from Lord Derby's estate. A far-sighted decision was taken to use the now-extended land at the eastern end of the campus as a main base for sports facilities, thereby liberating the former playing fields on the western side for potential future development.

In May 1997 the new £4m Sporting Edge facilities were opened by Mike Atherton, England cricket captain. The construction of the Sporting Edge building (incorporating a large multi-gym, squash court and fully equipped fitness suite), and associated upgraded six-lane running track, athletics facilities and floodlit

*The Sporting Edge facilities were opened by Mike Atherton, England cricket captain, in May 1997.*

*Overleaf: Students outside the Centre for Media, Information Systems and Technology (CMIST).*

all-weather and grass pitches, was part-funded by the Sports Lottery fund. The facility formed the base for the England Sports Council's North West regional training unit. The Sporting Edge was a facility for students, staff and the wider community (the first one in West Lancashire) and it helped greatly to cement Edge Hill's relationship with amateur and professional sport in the region, and with the community. The new facility was commended for its sensitive landscaping.

### Edge Hill Five Years After 'The Future of Higher Education'

By summer 1997, Edge Hill was considerably stronger than it had been five years previously. Despite a reduction in the unit of resource (the sum paid by funding councils for each full-time equivalent student) of 30 per cent, annual income had more than doubled to £24.3m, and a financial surplus had been made for each of the past four years. Undergraduate provision had grown significantly through the diversification afforded by the BA/BSc modular scheme. Initial Teacher Training was growing in strength: the College was now the largest national single-site provider of Primary ITT, while Secondary and Middle Years ITT provision was growing quickly. The School of Health Studies was increasingly integrated into College structures and was gradually diversifying its portfolio.

External reviews of the quality and standards by HEFCE, TTA and HEQC had revealed many strengths and no serious weaknesses, and the 1996 Research Assessment Exercise had yielded some encouraging results for the College. Over £21m had been spent developing the Ormskirk estate and its infrastructure. The College was developing a national reputation for its work in widening participation and its support for students.

But Edge Hill was vulnerable. A survey by the HEIST Marketing Consultancy, published in 1996, had revealed that although the College was valued by those who knew of it, levels of knowledge about it were generally low, particularly outside the region. Edge Hill was about to apply to HEQC for taught degree-awarding powers (TDAP), and was aware that its future use of the University College title was not guaranteed: the Principal noted in a paper for Governors in December 1996 that 'TDAP could be used as a formal criterion for the confirmation of university college status'. Change was in the air: the new Labour government was elected with a landslide majority in May 1997 and, a few weeks later, published Lord Dearing's *Report of the National Committee of Inquiry into Higher Education*, better and colloquially known as the Dearing Report. A new era was starting for universities and colleges.

# Development, Diversification and Disappointments

7

## The Dearing Report

The 1997 Dearing Report was the first major national report on higher education since the Robbins Report of 1962 and was published at a time when change was expected by all in the HE sector.

Dearing's report still reads well. Many of his recommendations – on increasing student numbers, on growing sub-degree provision and on promoting and supporting widening participation – had wide support across the sector. He set a demanding agenda for the new Quality Assurance Agency (QAA) in asking it to oversee the construction of an 'academic infrastructure' that would regulate the use of qualification titles (such as BSc or MA) through a higher education qualification framework. He proposed the development of a framework to allow credit accumulation and transfer between universities (a recommendation that was to take ten years to put into effect). He proposed that all universities and colleges should run a professionally accredited induction course for new teachers in higher education (it will be recalled that Edge Hill had been doing this for some years). But there were two particular recommendations that were of special significance to Edge Hill.

The first major challenge came as no surprise: full-time undergraduate students would start to make a financial contribution to their higher education studies. Recommendation 75 stated:

> *On a balance of considerations, we recommend to the Government that it introduces arrangements for graduates in work to make a flat-rate contribution of around 25 per cent of the average cost of higher education tuition, through an income contingent mechanism ... The contributions made by graduates in work in this way should be reserved for meeting the needs of higher education.*

The government accepted the 'flat-rate contribution' element of the recommendation but had already decided that this would be achieved through an up-front fee payable by full-time undergraduates, initially of £1,000, rising with inflation each year. This fee would be levied from September 1998. Although there were concerns about the effects on student recruitment, particularly from 'widening participation' institutions like Edge Hill (there was a modest sector-wide dip in applications in 1998), overall sector applications continued to rise year on year after then.

Another Dearing recommendation had an impact on Edge Hill and other colleges without taught degree-awarding powers (TDAP). The report proposed (recommendation 65) that:

> *The Government takes action, either by clarifying the legal position or by ensuring that conditions can be placed on the flow of public funds, to restrict the use of the title 'University College' to those institutions which are in every sense a college which is part of a university under the control of the university's governing body; and to those higher education institutions which have been granted taught degree-awarding powers.*

This principle was adopted in the government's subsequent Teaching and Higher Education Act. TDAP

Aerial view from the mid-1990s.

would therefore be necessary legitimately to retain the use of the University College title. This was Edge Hill's next challenge: it was to take rather longer to achieve than was originally envisaged.

### TDAP: An Early Setback

Edge Hill made its first application for TDAP in late 1997. In retrospect, it is now easy to see that this application was premature: while quality assurance systems and processes had been established, they had only been in effective operation for four years, and were not fully embedded across the institution. It was noted that the former polytechnics took 10 or 15 years working under the tutelage of the Council for National Academic Awards (CNAA) before they could reach an equivalent status. Following a panel visit and consultation with the Quality Assurance Agency (QAA), the institution agreed to withdraw the application and to resubmit at an appropriate stage in the future. An immediate casualty was the 'University College' title, which was withdrawn: a new corporate identity and logo, identifying the institution simply as 'Edge Hill', was introduced in 1999. Alongside the new corporate identity, the College developed a short but ambitious 'Vision Statement', setting out a vision of the institution in 2005. The statement began: 'By 2005 Edge Hill will be a thriving independent University College, which will support the development of students as rounded professionals, with high level of academic, professional and life skills and employability.'

The feedback from QAA suggested some lack of clarity in decision-making processes and structures across the College, in particular in the distinction between the 'collegial' or 'deliberative' processes of validation, evaluation and peer review through the

The new logo introduced in 1999, identifying the institution simply as 'Edge Hill'.

Academic Board and its committees, and the 'executive' processes of people and resource management. To address these comments, the College established a 'Committee on Committees', which reported early in 1999. The recommendations, accepted by the Academic Board, included a restructuring of the Academic Board committee structure, the establishment of 'Executive Groups' to oversee executive management functions, and the establishment of a new Academic Planning Committee, to oversee the development of the academic course portfolio. The revised structures were put into place for September 1999.

The development of quality assurance systems and processes across the College had reached the stage where senior academic oversight below Directorate level was necessary. A new post of Head of Quality Assurance and Standards was established in 1999: Professor Colin Raban from Sheffield Hallam University, an experienced QAA Auditor, brought a keen intelligence and fresh insights into institutional processes. Under Raban, the College was awarded £130,000 by HEFCE to develop a 'Quality Risk Management' project.

In 1999 an important and enduring means of communication was introduced: John Cater's (more or less) weekly email to staff across the institution. The email adopted a lively style: sometimes self-deprecating, sometimes humorous but always absolutely frank, topical and to the point in addressing, in an open and honest fashion, the key issues facing the institution, such as student recruitment and retention, quality assurance and relationships with major stakeholders. Student sports, staff achievements, other news items and events in the Rose Theatre were also covered. Often finished late on Friday afternoons, the email would not be complete without a geographically informed reference to the weekend weather prospects. With Cater's regular staff addresses at the start of each term, open to all, colleagues at Edge Hill were probably better informed about the major strategic issues facing the institution and the sector than educational staff anywhere else in the country.

### More External Academic Scrutiny

The post-Dearing settlement had seen responsibility for the HEFCE teaching quality assessment process moved to the QAA, who were now to operate the twin processes of subject review (as it now became) and institutional audit. The College entered an intensive period of external academic scrutiny from QAA, Ofsted, the English National Board for Nursing and Midwifery (ENB) and other professional bodies. Failure in any element of any inspection or review would have a disastrous effect on the prospects of gaining TDAP.

Over the next few years, the subject review cycle continued remorselessly, and outcomes improved considerably compared with the mid-1990s, with no scores under 20 (out of a possible maximum of 24). Mathematics and Sport achieved 20/24, Health and the new Psychology programme both achieved 22/24, Biology 23/24 and Education Studies, towards the end of the cycle in 2002, a maximum 24/24. The outcome for Health, endorsed by the ENB, was particularly satisfying as it established the School of Health Studies as the best in the Merseyside and Cheshire sub-region and set a strong basis for the further development of professional provision.

Under the Head of School of Education, Freda Bridge, the disappointing Primary Ofsted inspection outcome of 1997 was reversed, with strong inspection outcomes for both Primary and (with one or two exceptions) Secondary ITT. Following Bridge's departure in 2000, Robert Smedley, formerly Head of Mathematics, took over as Head of School, and the most successful period

in the School's history began: in 2003, Primary ITT was awarded a top grade for the Management and Quality Assurance of its provision – a rare accolade.

### Further Development of the Academic Portfolio

The late 1990s saw a period of rapid curriculum development across the five Schools as student numbers continued to grow: a strong emphasis was placed on the development of undergraduate provision which gave some form of professional accreditation. In 2000, the Psychology degree achieved accreditation by the British Psychological Society, and the new Journalism degree was recognised by the National Council for the Training of Journalists. A team was assembled to develop and deliver an LLB Law honours degree, which achieved professional accreditation from the Law Society in 2003. Other provision developed within the modular scheme in this period included programmes in Creative Writing, Film Studies, New Media, Information Systems, Childhood & Youth Studies and Marketing. But it was the department of Sports Studies and Physical Education that saw the most dramatic growth. From a position in the mid-1990s with only a small joint honours programme, the department developed a successful series of honours degrees, initially in Sports Studies, then Sports Science, Coach Education, Physical Education and Sports Therapy.

The late 1990s saw the continuation of the process of departmental rationalisation as student demand, stable in terms both of levels and subject mix in the 1980s and early 1990s, changed significantly from year to year. A market economy was developing in higher education, and a series of unviable courses: Community and Race Relations, Urban Policy Studies, Contemporary Religious Beliefs, Music and Art, were closed in the late 1990s. Early closures promoted fierce debates at the Academic Board, but by the end of the decade, course closures and a concomitant rapid pace of course development and renewal, was accepted as a necessary part of the new, demand-driven environment.

The Faculty of Education continued the period of growth initiated earlier in the decade. The secondary

*The Rose Theatre was built for Edge Hill drama students in the 1960s. Over the years it has hosted many touring companies and now over 75 productions take place each year.*

***Sue Smith, BSc (Hons) Sports Studies 1999–2003***

Sue Smith is one of England's most successful women's football players with 74 international caps and 14 goals, scoring against Germany on her debut appearance. She has twice been voted Nationwide International Player of the Year and was the sole England representative in the FIFA XI v US showpiece match in 1999. She currently plays for Leeds Carnegie Ladies and was one of the first female players to be awarded a central contract by the Football Association which allowed women footballers to be paid when playing for their country. Off the pitch, Sue is a commentator on women's games for BBC Sport and Sky Sports and recently worked with Wayne Rooney, presenting the player's *Street Striker* series on Sky TV.

PGCE portfolio was expanded to include all national curriculum subjects and beyond, with new programmes such as Music, Urdu and Citizenship being introduced. The 'Middle Years' programmes, piloted earlier in the decade and noted in the previous chapter, became a series of innovative 'Key stage 2/3' programmes. These were among the first in the country, straddling both primary and secondary education. The growth of these programmes, along with secondary provision, more than compensated for the temporary reduction in overall primary student numbers from 1999, when a bold decision was taken to reduce the length of the primary BA/BSc QTS programme from four years to three. The School, under its new Head, Robert Smedley, agreed a new contract for the Continuing Professional Development of teachers with the Teacher Training Agency in 2000. Robert Smedley, Dean of Education, comments:

> *One of our first major successes in terms of national contracts came in the form of INSET funding. This represented more than simply a substantial contract to deliver: it represented a change in how the School of Education would deliver Continuing Professional Development (CPD) for teachers. Historically CPD had been delivered in the form of face-to-face lectures and seminars with traditional assessments at the end of modules. This had to change if CPD was to have impact on teachers' professional practice in the classroom. The new contract was the way forward and would change the way accredited CPD was delivered by Edge Hill. The contract had been secured on the basis of new, strong partnerships with schools and local authorities and the portfolio of provision ensured impact in the classroom through practice-based masters level programmes. This one single project became a flagship model for accredited CPD and the recent Masters in Teaching and Learning (MTL) initiative originates from this school-based model.*

*Music teaching at primary level.*

In 2000, HEFCE announced a major initiative, arising from the Dearing Report. Large amounts of public funding were to be allocated to the development of 'Foundation Degrees', a new qualification broadly equivalent to the first two years of an honours degree, vocationally oriented and delivered substantially through the workplace. Bids for pilot schemes were invited, and the College persuaded Lancaster University, as the awarding body, to lead what became a successful consortium bid to HEFCE for development funding and additional student numbers. Building on its 'Specialist Teacher Assistant' (STA) experience, an important decision was taken to develop a foundation degree for Primary Teaching Assistants. The programme was promoted in March 2001 at a memorable open evening attended by 700 applicants: the programme recruited strongly in September of that year, and continues to run successfully, alongside a version for secondary teaching assistants, to this day. One of the features of foundation degrees particularly attractive to students is the ability to 'top up' a foundation degree to an honours degree, subject to appropriate levels of achievement. Many foundation degree students have, over the years, gone on to gain honours degrees, some achieving first-class honours. From 2002 onwards, other foundation degrees were developed across the College, many running at partner colleges of further education.

The School of Health Studies matched other areas of the College in terms of its academic developments. In 1998, through a competitive bidding process, the College was selected as the 'preferred provider' for nursing and midwifery training in the Cheshire and Merseyside sub-region. This resulted in increased student numbers and a new contract to provide pre-registration diploma and honours degree programmes for nurses, including, for the first time, training of children's nurses at Liverpool's Alder Hey Hospital. Another important development took place in 2001, when the College won a major contract through competitive tendering to deliver the Operating Department Practitioner (Theatre Technician) programme in Merseyside and in Greater Manchester. This outcome represented an important diversification of the School's provision, and also ensured a physical institutional presence in the capital of the North West region.

*Edge Hill University is one of the largest providers of training for health care professionals in the North West.*

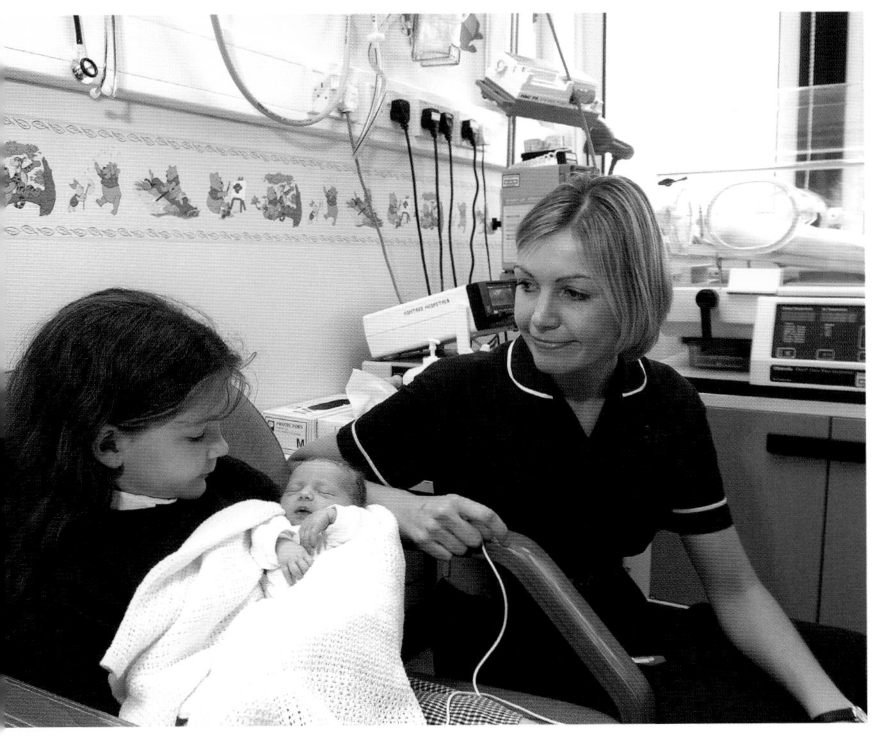

### Research Developments

The College's modest success in the 1996 Research Assessment Exercise (RAE) concealed an overall weakness in this area and the lack of a clear strategy to develop research across the institution. In 1997 the decision was taken to create a new senior post to lead the development of research, and Professor Alistair McCulloch, from Robert Gordon University, Aberdeen, was appointed. McCulloch skilfully used his training as a political scientist to raise the profile of research across the College: it would be fair to say that up to this point, research had been regarded by many academic staff as a voluntary activity, peripheral to what was commonly regarded as the main task of teaching and supporting undergraduate students.

An immediate target was the rate of completions of research students on doctoral programmes. A number of bursaries had been established in the early 1990s to support full-time research students, but completion rates had been poor. Through the Research Committee, McCulloch established a rigorous code of practice for the support and supervision of research students, and in 2001 an innovative postgraduate certificate programme was developed to provide accredited staff training and development in this area, leading in time to an improvement in completion rates. Part-time doctoral study routes were promoted and the number of registered research students rose steadily to over 50. For the first time, in the 1998 Strategic Plan, the College expressed a 'longer-term intention' to seek research degree-awarding powers (RDAP), and by 2003, 44 doctoral completions had been achieved across the College.

Increased investment into staff research was ensured. A Research Development Fund was created, allowing staff to bid competitively for financial support for specific research projects. The international research

*Emeritus Professor Rhiannon Evans, Pro Vice-Chancellor (students and external) 1994-2008*

'True to its roots in opening up professional opportunities to first generation women, Edge Hill has made a consistent and significant contribution to widening participation for more than a century. Working towards university status at Edge Hill over the last six or seven years, I was often reminded of the thrill and excitement I had felt as an undergraduate at Sussex University in the early 1960s, when we very aware that we were playing our part in creating the first of the new universities. And recently, I was delighted to find a link between Edge Hill and Sussex in the person of Helena Normanton (see page 36), who was an outstanding Edge Hill student in the early 1900s. Helena was a radical reformer in a number of spheres, the second woman to be called to the bar and the first to practise, later becoming one of the first woman KCs. She retired to Brighton where, in the late 1950s, she was the first benefactor of Sussex University and an outspoken and ambitious member of the board that oversaw its foundation. And so for me the wheel comes full circle.'

profile of the College needed raising, and an Overseas Travel Grant scheme was created, supporting staff giving papers at prestigious international conferences. Annual targets were set for academic departments for research outputs, such as books, refereed journal articles, conference papers and external funding. Dr John Archer of the History department was awarded £147,000 by the Economic and Social Research Council for his project on 'Violence in the North West of England from 1850 to 1914'. Scientists in the College, along with colleagues in Liverpool and Kingston Universities, were awarded £180,000 by the National Environmental Research Council to investigate 'High resolution lacustrine record of holocene climate change'.

Professorial awards had been available in the College since 1990, and a small but growing number of academic staff had been awarded professorial titles. Dr John Simons, at that stage Head of the School of Humanities and Arts, and Chris Parker, the Head of History, were awarded personal chairs for their scholarship, respectively, in English literature and History. The position of Reader was introduced, and over the years several academic staff progressed from Readership to Professorial titles. Alongside this, the position of 'Reader in Educational Development' was created to recognise excellent scholarship and research in students' learning, and a new Centre for Research in Teaching and Learning was established. That being said, overall progress in research was not as quick as many would have liked. The College entry in the Research Assessment Exercise (RAE) in 2000 showed only marginal improvements over the 1996 survey: the journey towards research excellence was to take more time.

### Consultancy and Knowledge Transfer

The late 1990s saw the start of a series of ventures in which staff research and scholarship were applied in a range of external settings. The Centre for Local Policy Studies, under its leaders Stuart Speeden and Dr (later Professor) John Diamond, developed its work significantly over this period. It completed a major study of the Race Equality Standard for the Commission for Racial Equality (CRE) in 2000, and in 2001 carried out a project evaluating the work of the Commission over the past 20 years. Resulting from this work, the Centre was commissioned to write an 'Equalities Standard' for a consortium consisting of the CRE, the Equal Opportunities Commission and the Disability Rights Commission.

### Teaching, Learning and the Internet

The late 1990s saw a massive growth in the application of the internet, in higher education as in other aspects of contemporary life. The College had ensured the physical infrastructure for these developments by continuing to invest in hardware and network technology, and as a founder member of Net North West (the regional IT infrastructure constructed by North West HE providers) it ensured high-speed connections to the Chorley Woodlands and the Aintree campuses alongside the main Ormskirk campus.

A far-reaching development was initiated in 1999 when the College was asked by the Mersey Deanery for Postgraduate Medical and Dental Education to develop an online postgraduate Certificate in Teaching and Learning in Clinical Practice, an innovative web-based distance learning course aimed at health practitioners who taught as part of their jobs. The first cohort, commencing in 2000, comprised 21 participants including 16 hospital consultants and registrars, four senior dental practitioners and one senior nurse. Participants met together for only four days a year but they could engage in debate through an online bulletin board at any time. The programme continues to prosper to the present day.

Developments such as this, and many others which followed in future years would have been impossible without a Virtual Learning Environment (VLE): software that facilitates web-based course delivery. In 1999, Edge Hill selected the widely used package WebCT as its VLE, and its use continues to the present day following WebCT's transition into the Blackboard VLE. By 2000, the College had around 1,000 students registered on programmes with some level of VLE presence: within a few years this had risen to the full student population.

In these early years, the College deliberately chose an organic approach in its development of 'e-learning', as it became known. A major stride was made in 2000 when the College was awarded HEFCE funding for the COMET (Communicating and Managing through the Educational Application of Technologies) project, led by the Head of Teaching and Learning Development, Dr Andrew Sackville and the Head of Library and Information Services, Ruth Jenkinson, who was replaced on her departure to Bolton University by the Deputy Head of Service, Sue Roberts in 2001. COMET's main aim was to deliver institution-wide change through the embedding of new technologies in teaching and learning: the first annual COMET project, held in 2001, was attended by over 90 delegates from 14 institutions.

### Supporting a Diverse Student Body

Under the leadership of the Director for Students and External Relations, Professor Rhiannon Evans, the period between 1997 and 2003 saw the College develop from a regional to a national leader in the widening of participation, in pursuit of the government target of 50 per cent participation in higher education. The first institutional Widening Participation strategy was approved in 1999. In that year, the College became the lead institution, with the three other Lancashire HEIs, for the Lancashire Compact: a three-year, £975,000 HEFCE-funded project focusing on widening participation in higher education in the county. The Compact aimed to identify barriers to higher education and to seek ways of overcoming them.

The College also became a lead partner, with the Liverpool HEIs, in the Merseyside Aimhigher project, with a particular institutional focus on raising the profile of science and mathematics with young people. ACE (Aiming for a College Education) days continued, with school pupils working with undergraduates. Along with a series of successful summer schools for Year 9-11 pupils, giving schoolchildren the experience of residing on campus and working with Edge Hill students, and

*Edge Hill prides itself on being a leader in the application of Information and Computer Technology (ICT) in support of students' learning.*

the six-week full-time Fastrack summer school, which by 2002 was recruiting over 100 students, the College was developing a range of approaches to encourage young people and adults into higher education. In 2003, Fastrack was supplemented by Fastforward, a part-time, work-based programme supported through WebCT, giving students direct access to a range of Edge Hill degrees. By 2000, the College had been identified by HEFCE, through its earmarked allocations, as the top performing HEI in England for widening access.

Success in this range of activities was further recognised when Edge Hill was appointed lead institution for Partnerships for Progression and for Summer Schools, on behalf of all 16 North West higher education institutions, developing the regional model for what would become Aim Higher from 2002. Evans was also appointed to the HEFCE-funded national coordination team for widening participation, serving as the as regional adviser for Yorkshire and the Humber, and promoting research and evaluation in access and widening participation.

As foundation degrees developed, it became clear that the many students in the region would benefit from commencing their higher education study in their local further education college. Accordingly, partnerships were developed with a series of local and regional colleges, starting with Knowsley Community College and Hugh Baird College, through which students could study the new two-year foundation degrees.

The importance of support for students with a range of disabilities and specific learning needs was increasingly recognised. The Teaching and Learning Development Unit was awarded a grant from the Staff Education and Development Association (SEDA) for assisting the increasing numbers of students with dyslexia to adjust to the expanding use of computer technology in College study. Full-time disability advisers and learning support officers were appointed, alongside a range of staff across the institution with specific responsibilities in supporting disabled students.

Edge Hill students were proving to be very employable. In 1998, the College was listed in the *Times*

*Edge Hill runs a Fastrack summer school to encourage young people and adults into higher education.*

*Higher Education Supplement* as the top institution in the country for the proportion of graduates entering employment after six months. Under Jacqui Howe's leadership, the College's Careers Centre was among the first to be awarded the prestigious Matrix accreditation in 2003.

### Development of the Estate

While the five years up to 1997 had seen some important developments to the Ormskirk estate, the years that followed saw the development and execution of a full, campus-wide Estates Strategy at Ormskirk. The land purchase of 1995 at the eastern end of the campus had released the former playing fields at the western end of the campus for development, and the first outline plans for the 'Western Campus' were presented to Governors in March 1999. The first building of the Western Campus was the £1.5m Business and Management Centre (BMC) in 1999, opened by the Duke of Gloucester, followed a year later by the striking £4m Learning Innovation Centre (LINC). The three-storey LINC building, the tallest on the Ormskirk skyline, provided a major focus for the work of the COMET project and its successors. It provided staff and students with over 200 open access computers and a state-of-the-art television and multimedia studio, and was opened in September 2000 by Sir Brian Fender, Chief Executive of HEFCE.

A group of wartime buildings, which for many years housed the department of Design and Technology, were demolished when the department moved, along with the Mathematics department, to a new £1.3m building, complete with workshops for textiles, electronics, graphics and computer-aided design, on the site of the former Levens building, adjacent to the Ruff Lane entrance. In their place, the new £3m CMIST (Creative Media, Information Systems and Technology) building was erected in 2003, housing the rapidly growing academic departments of Media and Information Systems. The Minister for Higher Education, Alan Johnson, in opening the building, pronounced himself 'gobsmacked', referring to Edge Hill as a 'well-kept secret'.

At the eastern end of the campus, accommodation was needed to support the rapidly developing Sports Studies and Sports Science degrees, and also to provide dedicated accommodation for Nursing and Midwifery students and staff at Ormskirk. It was necessary for this building to be sited adjacent to the new Sporting Edge building, and so the old Lancashire Hall student residential tower block on that site was demolished one summer weekend, providing some entertainment for the local community. The new £4.3m facility was opened in 2001 by Lord Derby, and was named the 'Wilson Centre' in honour of the recently retired and long-serving Chair of Governors, Bob Wilson. The building included high quality teaching space, IT suites, a large 300-seat lecture theatre (at that stage the largest in the College) and specialist laboratories for sports psychology, physiology and biomechanics, alongside a spacious dance studio. It was also the location for the new student health centre and counselling suite. The Wilson Centre was designed on 'green' principles to be environmentally friendly,

*The Learning Innovation Centre (LINC).*

*The Business and Law School, opened in 2008.*

making the maximum use of natural light and with a natural airflow ventilation system in teaching areas.

But the estate developments were not restricted to Ormskirk. The College entered into a partnership with the University of Liverpool and University Hospital Aintree for the development of the Clinical Sciences Centre for Research and Education: within this new building to operate the Learning and Information Research Centre (LIRC), the largest multi-disciplinary medical library in the North West Health Authority region. The LIRC is used by Edge Hill student nurses and midwives, alongside University of Liverpool undergraduate medical students, postgraduate researchers, staff employed by University Hospital Aintree, and for Edge Hill students it replaced the dated facility in the School's main building.

Edge Hill started to widen its network of what soon became known as 'outreach centres'. The Operating Department Practice contract for Greater Manchester necessitated premises in the city, and a base was established adjacent to St Thomas's Hospital in Stockport. After a few years, more central premises were leased in Gateway House, outside Piccadilly Station in central Manchester. The School of Education, in partnership with Cheshire LEA, formed its first outreach Teacher Development Centre for at Woodford Lodge, in Winsford, providing teachers in the county with opportunities for accredited continuing professional development.

The College also required a base in central Liverpool to deliver training and part-time vocational provision. A Business Learning Centre was established in Silkhouse

At work in a television editing suite.

Court on Tithebarn Street in the city centre, and the accommodation has formed a useful base for the institution's Merseyside-based activities since then.

### A Maturing Business

For many in higher education, the concept of universities and colleges as businesses would be anathema. Yet businesses they are: John Cater often remarked that high academic quality and standards must sit alongside high levels of financial stability, market awareness and staff commitment in order for the institution to continue to prosper. The period 1997–2003 saw annual income rise by 50 per cent to £36m: in each of these years, the College made a substantial surplus, rising to over £1.5m towards the end of the period. These surpluses were reinvested in the College's estate, thus allowing borrowing to be kept at a relatively modest level. Regular scrutiny by the sector's HEFCE auditors demonstrated high levels of financial probity within the institution. This financial stability was achieved at a time of frantic government activity, when each new minister sought to make his or her mark with a 'big idea'. Two such ideas: the NHS University and the e-University, promoted respectively by the Department of Health and HEFCE, were launched with a flourish in 2000 and 2001, and had disappeared two years later with little to show.

Even in the late 1990s, Edge Hill remained, in Alan Johnson's words, a 'well-kept secret'. In 2000, after much debate, the College developed its first television commercial, shown widely on regional networks. Other more sophisticated commercials followed at regular intervals after, each one playing its part in establishing the distinctive Edge Hill brand. The College, however, remained best known in the North West region, recruiting over 80 per cent of its full-time students from that area. In the immediate sub-region comprising the borough of West Lancashire and the six surrounding councils, with a population of 1.3m, Edge Hill was the only higher education institution.

The College's commercial company, Edge Hill Enterprises, had been a success story of the 1990s: by 2000, its turnover was exceeding £4m. Much of this income came through successful training and education projects funded through the European Social Fund (ESF). Levels of deprivation in Merseyside ensured that

*The CMIST (Creative Media, Information Systems and Technology) building was opened by Alan Johnson in 2004. It offers degree programmes in media production, journalism and computing, and provides students and staff with the very latest in new media technology.*

the region remained a European Union 'Objective 1' area, with higher levels of funding being available, and IT, business and management training programmes were successfully operated for several years, for clients including Royal Liver and Sony. However, in 2001 it became clear that ESF provision would no longer be financially viable, and a decision was taken to withdraw from European-funded work. Attempts were made to continue to operate IT and management training work on a full-cost basis, but there were too many regional players in a fiercely competitive market, and this provision was closed in 2005. Edge Hill Enterprises remains as a company, running the successful US 'study abroad' scheme.

The 'fourth leg' of business success, staff relations, continued to prosper over the period. The prestigious Investors in People (IiP) status was gained in 1998, and this award, indicating the College's strong commitment to staff development and training, was renewed successfully each following year. The College appeared in the top three of a national league table on equal pay for male and female employees, and in 2002 it became one of the first institutions to have its Human Resources strategy approved by HEFCE.

The College was fortunate in having a strong and committed Board of Governors to guide it through this period of development. Bob Wilson, who had chaired the Board with energy and purpose since incorporation in 1989, retired in 2000, and Robert Bradshaw took over as Chairman. As a partner with Coopers and Lybrand, Bradshaw had both the experience and the personal qualities to lead the Board and the College through its next stages of development, but in 2002 he was taken ill and died, at far too early an age, later that year. He

was succeeded as Chairman by the experienced Deputy Chairman, Brian Millner, a former senior manager at Pilkingtons in St Helens.

Under the Board of Governors, in 2001, the College's Mission Statement was subjected to its first major review in a decade. The revised Mission stated that 'Edge Hill is a Higher Education Institution seeking to provide an innovative, high quality and inclusive learning experience underpinned by a commitment to the advancement, dissemination and application of knowledge. Edge Hill is dedicated to developing individuals as skilled and autonomous learners in challenging and supportive environments.'

**Edge Hill and 'The Future of Higher Education'**
Taught degree-awarding powers (TDAP) continued to be an institutional imperative in order for the institution to be able to use the University College title, and thereby clearly to differentiate itself from colleges of further education. The old HEQC criteria had been revised by QAA and the Department for Education and Employment, and Edge Hill reopened its application for TDAP in 2001. Assessors were appointed by QAA, but following a disjointed series of visits and correspondence, the College was once again advised to withdraw its application in summer 2002. This came as a severe blow at the time, as the College this time felt fully ready to take on degree-awarding powers. If the first QAA referral in 1998 had seemed, in retrospect, understandable; the second one, four years later hit the College hard. Assessors noted some inconsistencies in terms of uneven academic leadership across the five Schools and in the College's administrative infrastructure. Action was necessary, as a

Students outside the Faculty of Education.

major government White Paper was due early in 2003, and it was widely expected that there would be further changes in the criteria for TDAP, research degree-awarding powers (RDAP) and University title.

During the winter of 2002–3, major changes in the academic structure of the College, the first for ten years, were therefore proposed, and, after fierce debate at two long meetings of the academic board, were approved (by a majority of one) and implemented over the forthcoming six months. While up to that time, the School of Education had overall responsibility for Initial Teacher Training (ITT), the three 'modular' Schools still held responsibility for some subject-specific elements of ITT provision. The emerging Ofsted inspection framework for ITT required a consistency in quality assurance arrangements for provision that could not be fully guaranteed across the four Schools. The argument that all ITT provision in any form be transferred to the School of Education, along with the transfer to Education of some 30 academic and administrative staff with responsibility for this work, formed the first of three major proposals from the Directorate. This was probably the most controversial of the proposals, as many academic departments such as English, History and Geography had their historic roots in ITT prior to the diversification of their provision.

The second proposal was the creation of three new faculties out of the five Schools. The now-enlarged School of Education became the Faculty of Education, The School of Health Studies (largely unchanged in structural terms) became the Faculty of Health, and the three other Schools combined to form the new Faculty of Humanities, Management, Social and Applied Sciences (HMSAS): this indigestible title was later changed to a more simple Faculty of Arts and Sciences. Each Faculty was to have a Dean and Associate Deans with defined academic leadership responsibilities.

The third strand of the proposals was the professionalisation of the academic administration across the institution, through the designation of a

HRH Princess Alexandra being shown around the Faculty of Education by Robert Smedley, 2004.

series of senior administrative posts in each faculty, the strengthening of the academic registry and the creation of a new post, the College Secretary, with overall responsibility for the further development of the College's administration. The College was fortunate in appointing Lesley Munro, an experienced senior administrator from the nearby University of Central Lancashire, to this post.

By late summer 2003, the building blocks for the revised College structures were in place. Three Deans of Faculty had been appointed: Professor John Simons in the Faculty of Arts and Sciences, Robert Smedley in Education and Eirlys Chinn, who had been Head of School (and the predecessor Sefton School of Nursing). Chinn retired in December 2004 and was replaced by Seth Crofts, who joined from Wolverhampton University. Munro was starting to draft new Academic Regulations for the institution. But the White Paper of January 2003, *The Future of Higher Education*, had signalled another series of major changes that would fundamentally affect Edge Hill and the rest of the sector. There would be a new application for TDAP, but another setback would be fatal.

Dancers in the Faculty of Arts and Sciences.

the wilson centre

# A Vision Realised

## 'The Future of Higher Education'

The January 2003 White Paper *The Future of Higher Education* proposed the fourth major set of structural and financial changes to the higher education sector in 15 years, largely put into effect through the fiercely debated Further and Higher Education Act of 2004. Several proposals in a wide-ranging paper were to have a profound influence on the higher education sector and on Edge Hill in particular. John Cater, who by then was chair of the Standing Conference of Principals (SCoP), recalls the period leading up to the White Paper as 'fascinating'.

As had been widely leaked, the fixed fee for full-time undergraduate students, then standing at around £1,200, was to be replaced a variable fee of '£0 to £3,000'. But the fee would not be payable upfront, as was the case with the current £1,200 fee: outstanding balances would be accumulated in the student's loan account, and repayment of the loan would only commence when their income level, following graduation, exceeded £15,000. No doubt the government hoped that a market would emerge in relation to the level of fees to be charged: in the event, however, all but one of the universities charged the full fee of £3,000, increasing annually with inflation. Universities and colleges were expected to use a proportion of the additional income generated to provide bursaries and scholarships to attract and support students: a new body, the Office for Fair Access (OFFA) was created to approve and monitor access agreements, a condition of charging higher fees.

There was more in the White Paper. Student grants would be reintroduced (albeit at a low level). Excellence in teaching would be recognised and promoted. But the biggest impact on Edge Hill came from the proposed revision to the criteria for taught degree-awarding powers (TDAP), research degree-awarding powers (RDAP) and University title. In simple terms, an institution that had achieved student number criteria (which Edge Hill met comfortably), met 'good governance' criteria, and had TDAP, would gain University title: the additional RDAP requirement would no longer be necessary. Within two years, several university colleges (already with TDAP) had successfully submitted applications for University title. Edge Hill could not be left behind.

## TDAP: the final instalment

The new criteria for TDAP were published in draft consultative form by QAA in September 2003, and the College agreed with QAA to submit an application for TDAP following their confirmation 12 months later. The broad opening statement of the criteria read:

> *An organisation granted taught degree-awarding powers is governed, managed and administered effectively, with clear and appropriate lines of accountability for its academic responsibilities. Its financial management is sound and a clear relationship exists between its financial policy and the safeguarding of the quality and standards of its higher education provision.*

Following the submission of the application in November 2004 and acceptance by the QAA's Advisory

Graduation, 2010.

Committee for Degree-Awarding Powers (ACDAP) that a prima facie case had been made, a team of assessors was appointed. This time, all went smoothly, with assessors busy with over 60 separate 'engagements' in the first half of 2005 involving meetings with groups of staff, Governors, external examiners and students, and the observation of a wide range of internal meetings. The scrutiny process concluded in July 2005, and a report recommending the award of TDAP made its way to the Privy Council in autumn 2005. The final report commented:

> *The attainment of taught degree-awarding powers has been a clear and longstanding strategic aim of the College over many years. The current application is accordingly the result of a sustained corporate strategy and its timing reflects Edge Hill's conviction that it has accumulated sufficient experience and maturity to exercise the responsibilities that accompany the grant of degree-awarding powers. The College has a strong academic community and the staff and students who met the institutional assessors were generally positive about their experiences at the College, many students drawing attention to the supportive and friendly learning environment.*

Edge Hill formally received confirmation of TDAP from the Privy Council office on 18 November 2005: a bottle of wine with a commemorative label was issued to all College staff.

Edge Hill was now immediately entitled to use the 'University College' title. But a greater prize was within grasp, and an extensive consultation exercise was quickly undertaken across the institution on the title that could be adopted if it was granted University title. Various alternatives were canvassed: 'West

*David Tomkins, Chair of Governors 2003–8*

'The invitation to consider joining the governing body of Edge Hill was, in the usual way of such requests, innocuously appealing and flattering, pointing to the occasional meeting and the opportunity to add something from my background in finance. It gave no hint of the volumes of reading needed for these meetings, nor that there already resided within the Edge Hill community substantial business awareness and expertise, to a degree unusual in Higher Education. Equally it gave no hint of the transformative experience I was to undergo in the following ten years, with the privilege of witnessing and having a small role in surely one of the most exciting periods in the Institution's long history.

The sequence of applying for and eventually being granted TDAP, RDAP and University title entailed extensive external scrutiny. Alarmingly, we discovered this included observing and examining the governing body and I for one was well out of my comfort zone facing academic questions from a panel of University Vice-Chancellors. Despite our best endeavours we did not derail the applications and the University received all the powers and status which its quality and achievements had long merited.'

Lancashire University' (too parochial?) and 'University of the North West' (which would almost certainly be opposed by all 16 other North West HEIs), and several others. Throughout the consultation, the simple and obvious choice of Edge Hill University remained a clear favourite, and early in 2006 the College duly applied to the Privy Council for this title, having also consulted with other universities and colleges in the region. The decision-making process for University title was decidedly unclear: Edge Hill was the first institution with TDAP under the new criteria to have reached this stage. After a nervous few weeks, and some deft footwork by Cater in heading off a potential and unnecessary review of financial governance by HEFCE, a letter was received on 18 May 2006 informing the institution that 'The Privy Council has modified the Instrument and Articles of Government of Edge Hill College, to include a change of title to 'Edge Hill University''. General rejoicing and another commemorative bottle of wine followed: fizz this time. The journey was completed – or was it?

### Research Degree-Awarding Powers (RDAP)

Well, no. In the last few weeks of 2005, with the certainty of TDAP, Edge Hill considered the possibility of applying for RDAP. Although research powers were no longer necessary for University title, Edge Hill wished to have parity of esteem with the other established universities in the country. Unlike most of the former polytechnics in 1992, however, it would have to fight for these powers. The December 2005 meeting of the Academic Board approved a proposal that the College should apply for RDAP during the next two years: the RDAP criteria were relatively new, and only one institution had gained research powers under them. Research infrastructure across the institution had been strongly developed, 60 students had been awarded research degrees over the years, and the number of professors and readers had grown, by external appointment and by promotion, to over 30. Following the TDAP success, Professor Colin Raban, Head of Quality Assurance, had departed and had been replaced by the new Dean of Quality Enhancement, Professor

Ian Robinson from Sheffield Hallam University. Levels of staff commitment and the will to gain RDAP were high. So, following consultation with QAA, a detailed application for RDAP was developed during 2006 and was considered by the QAA in December 2006 to have established a prima facie case. The development of the application entailed gathering detailed information on all staff research and scholarly outputs over a five-year period: in 2006 and 2007, the University knew more about the totality of its research activity than ever before.

Initially, the scrutiny progressed smoothly, with the now-familiar pattern of assessor 'engagements' running through most of 2007. A favourable draft report was submitted to ACDAP (Advisory Committee on Degree Awarding Powers) in December 2007, but the University had to endure more requests for detailed statistics on staff research and a final panel visit in June 2008, before the Privy Council confirmed that RDAP could be granted on 7 August 2008. Edge Hill University now had the same powers to award taught and research degrees as other universities. Mark Flinn, who as Pro Vice-Chancellor (Academic) had overseen these developments, retired in 2009, to be replaced by Professor Bill Bruce, formerly Deputy Vice-Chancellor of the University of Hull.

### Symbols of Status

Once the new University title was confirmed, a new corporate identity and logo was launched. Other changes and developments followed: the new University required a coat of arms, and the University Secretary, Lesley Munro, undertook discussions with the College of Arms in London. The resulting coat of arms, containing many images and symbols that reflected Edge Hill's history, along with the accompanying motto, *In Scientas Opportunitas* (In knowledge, opportunity) was unveiled in 2008. Professor John Simons, who devised the motto, recalls:

> *There was some debate as to whether a Latin motto (rather than one in English) was appropriate for a new university, especially one that had positioned itself with a strongly egalitarian mission to widen access to higher education. It was argued however that the motto had to transcend any particular period in the University's history and that the Latin actually enabled a happy ambiguity which was not available in English. It could imply either that Edge Hill offered opportunity to gain knowledge or that knowledge itself offered opportunity. The Latin thus enabled the University not only to capture its particular position at the time of adoption but also to make a general statement about the benefits of higher education which would endure for the future.*

Academic robes for graduating students and senior staff were designed, featuring the original Edge Hill colours of green and purple. A new mace, the symbol of the University's authority to award degrees, was commissioned from noted silversmith Clive Burr and was crafted in sterling silver with an 18-carat enamelled gold dome.

With the coming of University title, John Cater took the customary title of Vice-Chancellor, with the other

*The new Mace, designed by Clive Burr.*

*Coat of Arms*

The coat of arms consists of a shield, a crest, a badge and a motto and contains many images and symbols that reflect Edge Hill's history and values. The University's physical origins are represented by the red rose of Lancashire in the shield and by the Liver bird in the crest. While the red rose places the modern-day Edge Hill firmly in Lancashire, the Liver bird looks back to the institution's original location.

Edge Hill's ideological origins are present in the colours used in the coat of arms. The green and heliotrope (purple) are the colours of the suffragette movement and reflect Edge Hill's early commitment to the equality of women and its beginnings as a women-only college. Gold is associated with generosity and elevation of the mind.

The coat of arms is also full of symbolic objects and animals. The sun, seen in both the shield and the badge, represents illumination and enlightenment, the quill in the crest symbolises learning, while the peacock feathers stand for beauty, power and knowledge. Supporting the shield are a lion, representing strength, bravery and

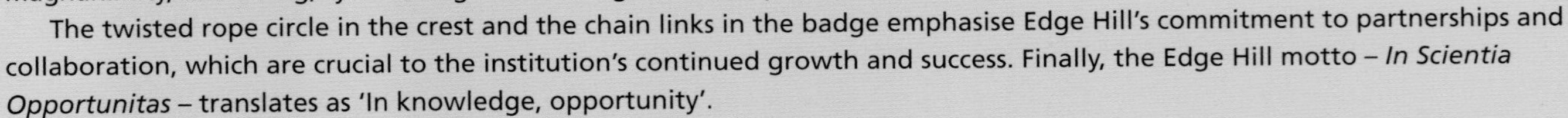
magnanimity, and a stag, symbolising wisdom, regeneration, peace and harmony.

The twisted rope circle in the crest and the chain links in the badge emphasise Edge Hill's commitment to partnerships and collaboration, which are crucial to the institution's continued growth and success. Finally, the Edge Hill motto – *In Scientia Opportunitas* – translates as 'In knowledge, opportunity'.

Directorate appointees becoming Pro Vice-Chancellors. But it was also necessary for the University to appoint a Chancellor: a well-known public figure who could represent and promote the University in the wider community and who would present academic awards to students at graduation ceremonies. The ideal Chancellor would be a woman, reflecting the roots of the institution and the 70 per cent female student body, with a professional interest in children and young people. Edge Hill was therefore very fortunate in 2008 when Dr Tanya Byron, the eminent clinical psychologist, author, policy maker and media personality, accepted the offer to be the University's first Chancellor. Dr Byron, soon appointed as a Professor of the University in recognition of her academic and public education role, has been an energetic, committed and enthusiastic Chancellor, tireless in her efforts to support the University and its students.

To assist the Chancellor in her role, two Pro-Chancellors were appointed. Christopher Trinick, Chair of the Qualifications and Curriculum Development Authority, who had been the Chief Executive of Lancashire County Council up to his retirement in 2008, was appointed to this role, alongside David Tomkins, who had been Chairman of the University's Governors since 2003. Following his retirement in 2008, Tomkins was replaced as Pro-Chancellor by the new Chair of Governors, Michael Pinfold.

The University was now ready to hold the first full ceremonies to award its own degrees. The new Faculty of Health building on the Western Campus could accommodate over 800 students, guests and staff, and the first graduation ceremonies were held in this building on 21 and 22 July 2008. At the first ceremony, the University was pleased to honour the achievements of Sir George Sweeney, the retiring Principal of Knowsley Community College, one of Edge Hill's strongest and longest-standing further education partner colleges, by awarding him the University's first honorary Master's degree, in recognition of his services to further education. Professor Tanya Byron was formally installed as Chancellor at the next ceremony on 6 December 2008, and Edge Hill awarded Professor Oliver Fulton from Lancaster University – a long-serving and recently retired member of the Board of Governors – an honorary Doctorate of Education in recognition of his distinguished academic record in higher education research and of his powerful and lasting contribution to Edge Hill's development. Other honorary degrees followed in 2009, including awards to the Edge Hill graduates, Sue Smith, the England footballer, and Stuart Maconie, the popular radio and television presenter, journalist and author.

The end of the decade saw the end of the formal degree-awarding relationship with Lancaster University. Edge Hill had many reasons to be grateful to Lancaster for its support and encouragement over the years, in particular for delegating sufficient responsibilities to

***Professor Tanya Byron, Chancellor***

'To be the first Chancellor of Edge Hill is an enormous privilege. I see my role as ambassador of the University, with a particular focus on being a public-facing and visible presence in order to spread the word about this jewel in the crown of Higher Education, tucked away in Ormskirk.

As a woman I feel particularly proud to wear the colours of the suffragette movement – purple, gold and green – when I am dressed in my exquisite ceremonial robes. These colours symbolise the auspicious beginnings of Edge Hill, 125 years ago, as the first non-denominational teacher training college for women.

Today Edge Hill continues as an institution dedicated to positive social challenge as we provide excellence without the elitism that is sadly still so endemic within the fabric of higher education. Our courses offer opportunities for high-achieving school leavers; adults wanting to return to education and either retrain or study; bright and enquiring young people whose previous educational experiences left them believing that they were unable to study for a degree. With a holistic agenda built around widening participation, Edge Hill enjoys an eclectic mix of students and staff offering a range of life skills and perspectives.

As Chancellor it has been my honour to shake the hands of our many graduands and bestow their degrees on them. To share their pride and joy – and to know that, as Edge Hill graduates, they will go onto achieve great things – is both overwhelming and humbling.'

*Professor Oliver Fulton, member of Board of Governors 1997-2006*

'Board meetings typically began with an exposition from Cater not only of current issues within Edge Hill but also of the wider context of national policy – and politics. It was an immense privilege to observe, and support, the steady emergence of a fully fledged University over the following years. Governing bodies generally hear, and worry, more about finance and real estate than about academic issues. It is to the Edge Hill Board's credit that while it respected the proper boundaries, it never lost sight of the academic and social mission – though for myself there was probably nothing to match the moments when the latest version of the campus master plan was presented, revealing the sheer scale of Edge Hill's determination to reinvent itself.'

the College, following accreditation in 1994, to allow it successfully to demonstrate its role as a responsible custodian of academic quality and standards. The last cohort of undergraduate students receiving Lancaster University awards graduated at Bailrigg on 17 July 2009, formally ending a mutually beneficial academic partnership which had lasted 35 years.

### Academic Developments

The late 1990s had seen a quickening of the pace of curriculum developments: this trend increased through the first decade of the new millennium. All three faculties saw significant developments as the University climbed into the third quartile of UK universities, according to the most widely used league table.

The Faculty of Arts and Sciences, under its Dean, Dr Nigel Simons, initiated a number of important developments. The new LLB Law degree prospered, and the Media department broadened its portfolio with new degrees in Advertising, Animation, Public Relations and Television Production Management, the latter drawing on a fruitful partnership with the BBC through its developing base in Salford. Probably the most significant development took place in the Department of Social and Psychological Sciences. In collaboration with the Faculty of Health, the Department successfully developed a professionally qualifying degree in Social Work, approved by the General Council for Social Care in 2008. This had been a long-term ambition of the institution, and added another major professional education and training route to the portfolio. Along with the thriving new degree in Dance, and a suite of Masters provision in Business and Management, the Faculty was prospering.

By the end of the decade, the Faculty of Education under Robert Smedley was probably the most successful such faculty in the country: it had been the biggest provider of Secondary Initial Teacher Training (ITT) for some years, and was now the largest provider of Postgraduate Professional Development (PPD), having

The Faculty of Education is now the country's largest provider of both Secondary Initial Teacher Training (ITT) and Postgraduate Professional Development (PPD).

gained a contract with the Training and Development Agency for Schools (TDA) for £11.5m over three years. Following a never-ending series of Ofsted inspections, the Faculty became one of a handful of providers, and by far the largest, to achieve the highest grade for the Management and Quality Assurance of both its Primary and Secondary ITT provision. Alongside this, the foundation degree provision for Teaching Assistants – noted in the previous chapter – had grown to include training for Higher Level Teaching Assistants. The Faculty diversified into the education and training of teachers and lecturers in the post-compulsory further education (FE) sector, through that extending the University's network of FE partners. It was also awarded a major £3.2m contract by the new Department for Children, Families and Schools, 'Every Child Counts', a numeracy intervention programme in Key Stage 1. The Faculty of Education was simultaneously envied and feared by many of its competitors across the land.

For years, the development of provision in the Faculty of Health had been held back by its physical location in University Hospital Aintree, ten miles

***Stuart Maconie, BA in English and Social Sciences 1979–82***

Stuart Maconie is an award-winning broadcaster, journalist, author, TV presenter and cultural commentator. Born in Whiston Hospital, Stuart grew up in Wigan where his parents still live. After graduation in 1983, he worked at Skelmersdale College as an English and Sociology teacher, before pursuing his dream career as a music journalist, landing a job at NME magazine where he eventually became deputy editor. The former Sony Broadcaster of the Year co-presents the *Radcliffe and Maconie Show* on Radio 2, as well as being a columnist for *Radio Times*, *Cumbria Life* and *Country Walking* and writing for *Word* magazine and *The Mirror*. He is a proud promoter of all things Northern and has penned two travel books, *Pies and Prejudice* and *Adventures on the High Teas*. He is currently working on a new book on British cultural history.

from Ormskirk. This came to an end in late 2007 with the completion of the new Western Campus Faculty building, initiating a series of collaborative developments with the other faculties. New provision in Women's Health, Health & Social Wellbeing and Health Sciences, alongside foundation degrees in Counselling and Public Health followed. A Masters programme in surgery was commissioned by Wrightington, Wigan and Leigh NHS Trust, aimed at senior medical staff with high-level skills, who sought to move to a consultancy role. The public reputation of the Faculty continued to grow following outstanding QAA and Nursing and Midwifery Council reviews throughout the decade. The year 2009 saw the next major development, with the gaining of a new contract to educate and train paramedic practitioners in Greater Manchester, thus giving the Faculty a fourth profession (alongside Nurses, Midwives and Operating Department Practitioners (ODP) with which to collaborate.

General view of the Western Campus.

With contracts for the training of both ODPs and paramedics in Greater Manchester, larger premises were necessary, and the new Faculty of Health outreach centre, Armstrong House on Oxford Road, opened in autumn 2009.

### Teaching, Learning and Research

The early years of the decade had seen the development of the institution's national reputation in e-learning (or blended learning, as it later became known), through the COMET projects. Following the January 2003 White Paper, HEFCE invited proposals for Centres of Excellence in Teaching and Learning (CETLs), and in January 2005, Edge Hill was one of only 20 per cent of bids awarded CETL status, to develop supported online and blended learning through its SOLSTICE (Supporting Online Learning for Students using Technologies for Innovation and Communications in their Education) project. Under its Director, Sue Roberts (Dean of Learning Services) and its Academic Director Professor, Mark Schofield (Dean of Teaching and Learning Development), SOLSTICE quickly gained an international reputation for its innovative research and development work, with its annual conferences attended by delegates from all six continents: the SOLSTICE model has proved to be both influential and enduring. The project influenced practice across the University when a decision was taken in 2007, under the new Dean of Learning Services and SOLSTICE Director, Alison Mackenzie, to ensure that all undergraduate provision was to have a defined Virtual Learning Environment presence. SOLSTICE 'hubs' were developed to assist foundation degree students in partner colleges to access high quality learning materials.

With research degree-awarding powers ensured, research outputs continued to develop across the institution. New research centres were established in Widening Participation (led by Pro Vice-Chancellor

An ODP student training at Edge Hill.

*Sue Roberts, Head of Learning Services 2000–08*

'Edge Hill was, and still is, a place that enabled and encouraged innovation… I learnt at Edge Hill that it was more than OK to 'fight above your weight', that you can and should dream big and not be confined by either history or by others' perceptions of you. This applied to Edge Hill's own growth on the local, national and international stage – resulting in the creation of a new University and SOLSTICE – and also to my perceptions of myself, and of what is possible. I hope that Edge Hill's graduates share this feeling of possibility and growth, and that it continues to inspire the University community as it continues to inspire me'

Professor Rhiannon Evans), Evidence-based Practice (Professor Barbara Jack), Learner Identity Studies (Professor Martin Ashley) and Sports Law Research (Professor Richard Parrish). A series of inaugural professorial lectures became a regular feature of term-time academic life, with intriguing titles such as 'Holy Mackerel, Batman' (Professor Kevern Verney) and 'Snooping Around: Adventures in Literary History' (Professor Harriet Devine).

The outcome of the 2008 Research Assessment Exercise (RAE), in which the University entered staff in six academic areas, indicated some world-class work in History and Nursing, and internationally excellent work in all six areas: this was a respectable result after the relatively disappointing 2000 RAE. Research at Edge Hill was no longer a voluntary 'cottage industry': it was an integral part of institutional life, with over 40 Professors and Readers.

### Students and Partnerships

The designation of Edge Hill as a University in 2006 greatly strengthened its attractiveness to students: applications grew by 40 per cent in the next academic year, following a generally upward trend over the decade. Total student numbers across the institution in the first decade of the new millennium rose from 8,900 to over 23,000. Students were better informed than ever on the choices available between institutions: a major change occurred in 2006, with the publication of the first National Student Survey (NSS), a single annual questionnaire survey completed by final-year undergraduate students in 141 institutions across England, Wales and Northern Ireland. Edge Hill performed well in this and subsequent surveys: in the first survey, teaching in Law was rated as the best in the country. A year later, the institution was ranked in the top 20 of English universities for overall student satisfaction, with eight subjects rated as the best in the region. Edge Hill has consistently finished in the top two institutions in the North West for student satisfaction, and in 2009 the website Whatuni.com rated the University in the UK's top ten for courses and lecturers.

In 2006 the new undergraduate fee of £3,000 was introduced. Edge Hill's innovative package of bursaries, scholarships and other awards was rated as one of the most generous in the country, winning the *Times Higher* award in this category that year. The package of bursaries encouraged students from non-traditional backgrounds to access higher education, while 'excellence scholarships' rewarded students with high levels of achievement in areas such as volunteering, creative and performing arts, and academic achievement. Under Christine Coleman, Director of Student Services, the University's reputation for high levels of support and guidance for students continued to prosper. A greater prize was achieved in the next *Times Higher* awards ceremony in 2007, when the University was short-listed, along with five others, for the prestigious 'University of the Year' award, a feat repeated three years later.

One issue, however, gave the University some cause for concern. Up to the late 1990s, undergraduate student retention and completion rates had been excellent, but the period from 2000 saw some deterioration in retention rates in Edge Hill as in other institutions, which, although just below sector norms, was well below the high standards that the University set itself. Benchmarking with other institutions demonstrated that there was no single solution or 'magic bullet' to tackle a complex and multidimensional problem. Ensuring greater numbers of student residential places would certainly help students to identify, and develop a long-term commitment, with the University, and, as described below, this was achieved, against some local council opposition, towards the end of the decade.

The University's regional and national leadership in widening participation continued through the decade under Pro Vice-Chancellor Professor Rhiannon Evans' leadership. The institution continued its leadership of the Aimhigher: Partnerships for Progression programme in the North West up to the closure of the regional office in 2008: Aimhigher organised a wide range of activities aimed at raising awareness and aspiration among schoolchildren from areas with historically low rates of participation in higher education.

In 2005, Edge Hill won the contract to be the lead institution for the national coordination and management team, Action on Access, which was established by HEFCE to coordinate and promote its widening participation strategy through collaborative projects and research into policy and practice: Evans was appointed as National Director, and the University's contract to run Action on Access was renewed for a further three years in 2009.

A major development came in 2006 when the University was approved by HEFCE as the lead institution for one of the country's first Lifelong Learning Networks (LLNs). LLNs focus on progression into and through vocational education: they aimed to create new learning opportunities; forge agreement across institutions on how qualifications are valued; and produce publicity to help people understand how they can progress through the system. Edge Hill became the leader of the Greater Merseyside and West Lancashire LLN, and over the next few years, working closely with Liverpool University, built a wide network of partners to ensure learner progression routes from FE vocational qualifications to higher education, often through Edge Hill foundation degrees offered at partner colleges. Both within and outside the LLN, the network of partners and outreach centres spread from the Isle of Man to east Lancashire, Greater Manchester, Cheshire and Shropshire.

*Christine Coleman, Director of Student Services*

'One of the great pleasures of the job is the enjoyment that comes from working with our students. We take delight in their successes obviously, but also in their sense of fun, their enthusiasm and vitality. For example, there is the annual Almost Nude Sponsored Run, which a former student, now a member of staff, has been organising since his first year at University. Not an event for the fainthearted, this takes place on the last Wednesday of the winter term, when a group of students, staff and members of the public, in varying degrees of nudity, run a route around Ormskirk to raise money for charity.'

Following the granting of University status in 2006, Edge Hill was determined to develop its international profile, which up to then had mainly comprised a long-running US 'study abroad' scheme and a series of research and project links with European universities. Professor Rhiannon Evans, now with an MBE in the New Year's Honours list, retired in 2007 (retaining her Action on Access directorship) and in her place, Dr David Law, formerly International Director at Warwick University, was appointed. Law used his skills and networks to broaden the range of the University's international partners and to increase international student recruitment. Edge Hill Business and Management degrees were offered at Feiyang Institute of Technology, Singapore, and advanced nursing qualifications were developed for hospital authorities in Hong Kong. Students from West Africa, India and the Far East were recruited to the Business School's new MBA programme, and active research and consultancy partnerships were developed with the University of Johannesburg and with the Maldives. The University's first International Strategy plan was approved by the Academic Board in 2009, and the new Centre for International Education developed a unique MA in the Management of International Higher Education, which had its first intake in January 2010. The University was steadily growing its international presence and reputation.

### The Ormskirk Estate

While the basic concept of the Western Campus development had been initiated in the late 1990s, its final execution took some years to reach completion. The space between CMIST, the (then) Business and Management Centre and the LINC was fashioned into an attractive piazza, and a virtue was made of some poor drainage in the old playing fields to the west of this space by the creation of an attractive lake, with careful environmental design features overseen by Dr John Hindley, one of the institution's first biology doctorates, then working as Environmental Manager for the University's Estates Department.

Around the lake, two major buildings were constructed. The £9m Faculty of Education building – with 24 teaching rooms, a lecture theatre seating 300 students, accommodation for 100 staff and a lakeside-view café – was opened by Her Royal Highness, Princess Alexandra, in 2004. Three years later, the stunning £14m Faculty of Health building allowed most faculty staff to relocate from Aintree to this state-of-the-art facility. Partitions between the three large lecture theatres within the building could be removed to accommodate the degree ceremonies described earlier in this chapter. The new building featured many 'green' attributes, including space heating via a ground source heat pump system, and solar water heating, and was formally opened in June 2008 by Professor David Eastwood, Chief Executive of HEFCE. Later in 2008 it was shortlisted in the annual *Times*

*A piazza was created between the Business Management Centre and the LINC.*

*The Faculty of Health building opened in 2007. A lake was created in front of it on an area which was once playing fields.*

*Higher* Education awards ceremony for 'Outstanding contribution to sustainable development' (the third time in the first three years of the ceremony that the institution had been shortlisted for an award), and in the following year won a top Sustainability prize in the West Lancashire Design Awards and the RICS North West Sustainable Building of the Year award. The planning, development and completion of the Western Campus, executed over ten years by John Cater, the Pro Vice-Chancellor Steve Igoe and Director of Estates David Oldham, was a major achievement that greatly contributed to the regional and national reputation of the University, and its attractiveness to students.

The move of the Faculty of Education to the Western Campus vacated the old two-storey building adjacent to the Rose Theatre. The expansion of undergraduate numbers in Dance, Drama and

*The 'live energy wall' located in the main entrance of the Faculty of Health. As energy is used, the wall changes colour, reminding staff and students to turn off computers, lights and other electrical equipment after use.*

Performing Arts necessitated additional facilities. In 2005/06, this building, along with the nearby former Arts and Sciences building and the Rose Theatre itself, was remodelled as a major centre for the Performing Arts, comprising, alongside the Rose, a new studio theatre, a fully sprung dance studio, an atrium lobby and exhibition space, and enhanced studio space for production and construction work. The studio formed a base for the new 'Short Cuts' film society, giving Ormskirk its first public cinema screen for many years.

The transition between the central and western campuses was completed in January 2009 by the construction of the striking £8m Business and Law School, overlooking the now fully pedestrianised central piazza area. The consequential move of law and business staff allowed the 1999 Business and Management Centre to be refurbished, and substantially improved, for occupancy by the Department of Social and Psychological Sciences.

The final major construction project of this fruitful decade was to be the much-needed expansion of student residential facilities. Full-time student numbers had grown steadily over the decade, overseas student numbers were increasing, and the number of residential places had fallen by 100 when Lancashire Hall had been demolished ten years previously. The University applied to the planning authority, West Lancashire District Council (WLDC) for permission to demolish the former Director's house, along with the Ethandune building and the 1950s bungalow on St Helens Road, and to construct on their plot 240 new student residential places. WLDC initially (and inexplicably) twice refused planning permission for the full development, but on appeal to the Planning Inspectorate the decision was reversed, and the resulting 'Founders' Court' residences, named after six of the original 1885 founders, were opened for students in September 2009. A further 140 residential places behind the Education building was completed in August 2010. Along with the construction at the rear of the campus of a new building for the University's Facilities Management and IT Services Departments, and an additional gymnasium and sports therapy laboratory, the pace of development has not lessened.

The future development of the University into the next decade will be at the eastern end of the campus. In 2006, 84 acres of green belt farmland were purchased from the Lord Derby estate: the University now had ownership of all the land to the east of the University up to Scarth Hill Lane. The 1990s acquisition had supported the expansion of sports pitches into the green belt, an appropriate and permissible use of such land. Permission was sought for the further expansion of sports and associated facilities further into the green belt, linked to plans to construct a new campus entrance 500m to the east of the current entrance (thereby removing major rush-hour traffic problems at the original entrance).

*Founders' Court.*

Following the major Planning Inquiry in 2006, the Inspector, in his Report, while not giving immediate approval to the plans, expressed positive views about the longer-term potential for the University and WLDC to collaborate in the future development of this land, for the benefit of the University and the wider community.

### The University of Choice

The University prospered throughout the first decade of the new millennium. By June 2010 there were over 16,000 undergraduate applications to study at the University: more than in 40 other universities, five times as many as in 2000. Institutional income rose from £27m in 1999–2000 to almost £83m in 2008–9, and annual surpluses were made each year, rising to almost £9m (prior to accounting adjustments) at the end of the period. The student population rose to over 23,000. The HEFCE Quinquennial Review of 2008 had no recommendations or points for action. The University had ensured, through a tight and rigorous budget-setting process, and through the prudent management of resources, that it could continueto invest in improving the infrastructure and the student experience: in the period 2000–10, a total of over £100m had been invested in developing the Ormskirk campus.

A growing sense of confidence about the institution informed the development of the new Strategic Plan for 2008–15, in which the University set out its vision as:

> *...a leading university of choice for students and staff in the region. As a learning-led university, it will be acknowledged for its excellence in supporting student learning, for its excellence in teaching, learning, research and advanced scholarship and for its continuing capacity for organisational learning and development.*

*The Performing Arts Centre includes two theatres, dance and drama studios, seminar rooms, facilities for music as well as production studios for costume and scenery construction and computer-aided set design.*

*Left: A student drama production presented in the Rose Theatre.*

The University was becoming better known, regionally and nationally, following years of investment in the marketing of the institution under its Director of Marketing, Roy Bayfield. The innovative animated television commercials, featuring the engaging 'student', Jez, were introduced in 2005, and went on to win a series of awards. In 2008, the Council for the Advancement and Support of Education (CASE) awarded Edge Hill its Gold Medal for the creative uses of technology and new media, in recognition of 'Hi', the University's undergraduate applicants' website.

As a 'University of Choice', Edge Hill had to be attractive to both students and staff. Annual staff surveys, along with the continuing Investors in People recognition, demonstrated increasing levels of satisfaction with Edge Hill as an employer. A test of this came in 2006 when the University, in line with the rest of the HE sector, sought to implement the new pay framework agreement, introducing a common pay spine for all staff across the institution. A ballot of staff across the institution in summer 2006 showed overwhelming levels of support for the proposals, but there was a tense period of a few weeks in the autumn when the academic staff union, the Universities and Colleges Union (UCU), failed to follow the other staff union in endorsing the University proposals. Agreement with the UCU branch, however, was duly reached late in the year, and notwithstanding the decision of some staff (unsuccessfully) to seek to challenge its implications in the courts, the new pay framework has operated successfully and equitably since then. As if to confirm this, the University was rated by its staff in the top 20 of 'Best places to work in the public sector' in a survey conducted by the *Sunday Times* in 2010.

## Culture and Community

The University's cultural footprint grew significantly over the decade. The enlarged Performing Arts complex saw a diversified programme of theatre, film, music and comedy in the Rose and Studio theatres. By 2009–10, there were 80 professional productions in the Rose, and the annual summer visits of the 'Illyria' company, performing Shakespeare plays in the Rock Garden, were keenly anticipated, giving the University an opportunity to host friends and guests in the most attractive corner of the campus. June Gibbons, Rose Theatre manager, recalls:

> *A highlight of the summer season is an outdoor Shakespeare performance. We are usually lucky with the weather but there was one very memorable year when the ducks joined the actors for a spot of audience participation on the waterlogged and sinking stage. But rain did not stop play and even though the wind carried the actors' words off into the distance, the audience stoically sat it out in typically British fashion.*

*Helping children in the gym during teacher training.*

The 'Short Cuts' film season in the Studio Theatre prospered. From 2007, the University has sponsored a Short Story prize, awarded for new short story collections: prize-winners have included Colm Tóibin, Claire Keegan and the science fiction writer Chris Beckett. The distinguished author Hilary Mantel chaired the first panel of judges.

In the area of film and media, Edge Hill's Emeritus Professor and distinguished Polish film director, Tomasz Pobóg-Malinowski, ensured the development of links with the Polish Film School in Ĺodz, and Edge Hill students have entered films in the prestigious annual student film competition held there. Malinowski's own photographs of Lancashire and India continue to grace university corridors.

The growing Arts profile was a facet of the University's investment in, and commitment to, the local community. In 2008–9, professional productions in the Rose Theatre were attended by 14,000 people, while a further 12,000 members of the community were active participants in either workshops or performances. The 2007–8 Annual Report noted that 'More than 400 students and staff volunteers supported some 80 local organisations, working on everything from conservation projects to charity collections.' Alongside the community health and fitness role of the Sporting Edge, the University's wider contributions to the community were becoming increasingly recognised.

An underpinning theme in the development of both the Rose and Sporting Edge has been term-time and holiday programmes aimed at local children, as part of the University's commitment to widening access. The Students' Union has also continued to play an important part in town and gown relations: developing one of the earliest Community Action schemes in the country, it has run a wide range of voluntary schemes every summer to provide extra support to children, families, people with disabilities and the elderly.

For the last 12 years, several local liaison groups have been given service by the University. A local residents' group meets regularly to discuss and share issues as they impact on the University and the town.

Members include local residents, representatives of the local police, landlords, the Student Union and senior members of the University, and a twice-yearly newsletter is delivered to all households and business in the neighbourhood.

The University has brought significant benefits and opportunities to the town of Ormskirk and wider communities in a number of significant respects: there are amenities such as a wide choice of restaurants, a bookshop and retail outlets, which simply did not exist even ten years ago. It has also helped thousands of landlords let vacant properties that, 15 years ago, gave real concern to the District Council when they were vacant. But, inevitably, the expansion of the campus has brought with it some tensions from time to time, which the University has always sought to mitigate with dialogue and active engagement.

### Towards 2135?

The University entered the second decade of the new millennium at a time of crisis for the economy and the higher education sector. The short-lived Department for Innovation, Universities and Skills (DIUS), created in 2007, was absorbed less than two years later into the new mega-Department of Business, Innovation and Skills (BIS) under the ubiquitous Lord Mandelson. For the first time, there was no government department with a title containing the words 'education' or 'universities'. The 'Higher Ambitions' plans from the BIS Department, launched in November 2009, committed the government to encouraging more competition between universities, giving greater priority to courses that meet the need for 'high-level skills'. Businesses would be encouraged to fund and design programmes and sponsor students and work placements, and more part-time and work-based routes through vocational programmes would be developed. While these developments were consistent with much of Edge Hill's developments over the past 20 years, collectively the plans presented what many in the sector regarded as a narrow and instrumentalist view of the role of higher education.

The greed and irresponsibility of bankers, and the failure of regulatory systems, had precipitated an 18-month economic recession, and public expenditure came under pressure as huge sums of public money were injected into the banks to ensure their survival. Expenditure in schools and hospitals was protected, and during 2009 it became clear that significant cuts would be made in the higher education budget. Over the 2011–14 cycle of the government's comprehensive spending review, cuts of over 25 per cent are expected: Cater's report to Governors in January 2010 commented that 'cuts on this scale and intensity have not been seen in UK HE for more than 25 years'.

Another major development in 2010 will be the outcome of the government's review of University tuition fees, chaired by Lord Browne, formerly Chief Executive of BP. The 2004 settlement had resulted in virtually all institutions charging full-time undergraduates the maximum allowable annual fee, which had risen by 2010 to £3,290. This outcome, however, satisfied neither those who wished to create a genuine fees market, nor those in the elite universities that claimed poverty under the current level of fees. The outcome of the tuition fees review, to be published after the 2010 General Election, will influence the higher education landscape for years to come.

For the past 17 years Dr Cater, as Principal and Chief Executive, and (from 2006) as Vice-Chancellor,

*Playing pool in The Venue.*

*Edge Hill University marked its 125th anniversary with a civic reception at Liverpool Town Hall.*

has led Edge Hill with distinction. He has overseen the transition of the institution from a vulnerable college of higher education to a confident and distinctive university. He has ensured the development of a culture in which the contributions of all colleagues were valued.

The national respect in which Edge Hill is held is, in no small measure, due to John Cater's outstanding leadership and his long-term vision for the institution. He has met the many challenges facing the institution with personal integrity, good humour and impeccable judgement, informed by an unrivalled understanding of the forces that drive and change the higher education sector. His public service, as Chair of the Standing Conference of Principals, and with the Teacher Training Agency, the Quality Assurance Agency, Universities UK and the Higher Education Careers Service Unit, has made a strong contribution to the development of Edge Hill's national reputation. The University, as at many other times in the past 125 years, has been fortunate in its choice of leader.

The University is confident about its future. The vision of learning initiated by the founders in 1885 has been richly realised. A dinner in Liverpool Town Hall in January 2010 celebrated the establishment of the institution in the Edge Hill district 125 years earlier. In many ways, the University has remained faithful to its roots: over 70 per cent of its students are women, over 80 per cent of undergraduates leave the institution with a professional qualification and Edge Hill still has provision for the caring professions at its heart. But it has gained in recent years the capacity and confidence to anticipate and adapt quickly to change, and that capacity will help to ensure the institution's continuing success. Those present in Durning Road in 1885 might have predicted the continuing success of Edge Hill 125 years later, and who now would deny the University at least another 125 years?

*Overleaf: Graduation, 2010.*

# Index

Where entries refer to academic courses all initial letters are Higher Case eg African History, Animation etc rather than African history, animation.

Illustrations are denoted in **bold**.



*Camila Batmanghelidjh, founder of children's charity The Kids Company, was a guest lecturer in 2010. Shown here with Chancellor Professor Tanya Byron.*

*Edge Hill alumni celebrate the University's 125th anniversary, 2010.*